A WORLD WIDE RAVE!

What the heck is that?

A World Wide Rave is when people around the world are talking about you, your company, and your products. Whether you're located in San Francisco, Dubai, or Reykjavík, it's when global communities eagerly link to you stuff on the Web. It's when online buzz drives buyers to you virtual doorstep. And it's when tons of fans visit your Web site and your blog because they genuinely want to be there.

RULES OF THE RAVE:

NOBODY cares about your products (except you).

NO coercion required.

LOSE control.

PUT DOWN roots.

CREATE triggers that encourage people to share.

POINT the world to your (virtual) doorstep.

**You can trigger a World Wide Rave too
—Just create something valuable that people want to share,
and make it easy for them to do so.**

WORLD WIDE RAVE

Creating triggers that get millions of people to spread your ideas and share your stories

David Meerman Scott

WILEY

John Wiley & Sons, Inc.

This one is for my brothers,

Alan and Peter.

CONTENTS

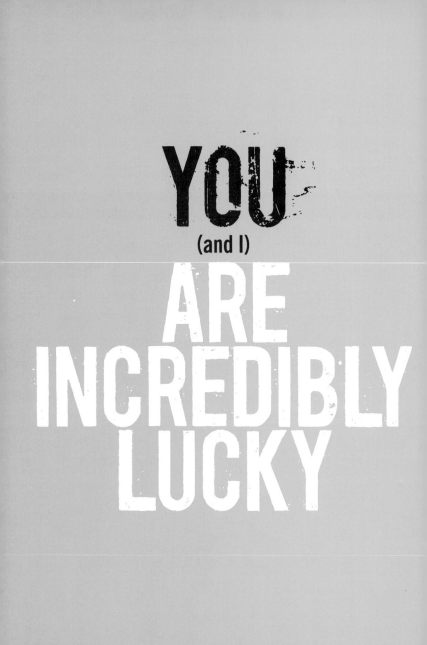

We're living in a time when we can reach the world directly, without having to spend enormous amounts of money on advertising and without investing in huge public relations efforts to convince the media to write (or broadcast) about our products and services. There is a tremendous opportunity right now to reach buyers in a better way: by publishing great content online, content people *want* to consume and that they are *eager to share* with their friends, family, and colleagues.

One of the coolest phenomena on the Web is that when an idea takes off, it can propel a brand or company to seemingly instant fame and fortune—*for free.* Creating a *World Wide Rave* in which other people help to tell your story for you is a way to drive action. One person sends it to another, then that person sends it to yet another, and on and on. Each link in the chain exposes your story to someone new, someone *you* never had to contact yourself! It's like when you're at a sporting event or concert in a large stadium and somebody starts "the wave." Isn't it amazing that *just one person* with an idea can convince a group of 50,000 people to join in? Well, you can start a similar wave of interest online, a *World Wide Rave*. You can create the triggers that get millions of people to tell your stories and spread your ideas.

A WORLD WIDE RAVE

The World Wide Rave is one of the most exciting and powerful ways to reach your audience. Anyone with thoughtful ideas to share—and clever ways to create interest in them—can become famous and find success on the Web. The challenge for marketers is to harness the amazing power of the World Wide Rave. The process is actually quite simple; anyone can do it, including you. However, if you're already an experienced marketer, you need to know that success requires a far different approach than what you're likely doing now. Many of the easy techniques for triggering a World Wide Rave are the exact opposite of what you've learned on the job or have been taught in school. Similarly, if you're a CEO, business owner, or entrepreneur, you should know that these ideas are likely precisely what your agency partners and marketing staff tell you *not* to do.

If you've already had some success getting your stories and ideas to spread online, great! Those experienced with online media will benefit from the wealth of new ideas and fascinating stories of success I share in these pages. There are some very surprising approaches here, and I believe even experts will learn a great deal.

So without further ado, let's look at the important components for generating a World Wide Rave of your own. As you read the next few paragraphs, consider how completely different these ideas are from what you're likely doing today.

RULES OF THE RAVE

Of course, it's obvious as hell that in order for thousands or even millions of people to share your ideas and stories on the Web, you must make something worth sharing. But how do you do that? Here are the essential components.

This list is so important, and each item such a strong predictor of success, that I call them your Rules of the Rave. I introduce the six rules here and then provide much more detail later, elaborating on each one in its own section of the book.

1. Nobody cares about your products (except you). Yes, you read that right. What people do care about are themselves and ways to solve their problems. People also like to be entertained and to share in something remarkable. In order to have people talk about you and your ideas, you must resist the urge to hype your products and services. Create something interesting that will be talked about online. But don't worry—because when you're famous on the Web, people will line up to learn more and to buy what you offer!

2. No coercion required. For decades, organizations of all kinds have spent bucketfuls of money on advertising designed to coerce people into buying products: Free shipping! This week only, 20 percent off! New and improved! Faster than the other guys! This product-centric advertising is *not* how you get people talking about you. When you've got something *worth sharing*, people will share it—no coercion required.

3. Lose control. Here's a component that scares most people silly. You've got to lose control of your "messages"; you need to make your valuable online information totally free (and freely sharable); and you must understand that a World Wide Rave is not about generating "sales leads." Yes, you can measure success, but not through business-school Return on Investment (ROI) calculators.

4. Put down roots. When I was a kid, my grandmother said, "If you want to receive a letter, you need to send a letter to someone first." Then when I was in college, my buddies said, "If you want to meet girls, you have to go where the girls are." The same thing is true in the virtual world of the Web. If you want your ideas to spread, you need to be involved in the online communities of people who actively share.

5. Create triggers that encourage people to share. When a product or service solves someone's problem or is very valuable, interesting, funny, or just plain outrageous, it's ready to be shared. To elevate your online content to the status of a World Wide Rave, you need a trigger to get people talking.

6. Point the world to your (virtual) doorstep. If you follow the Rules of the Rave as I've described them, people *will* talk about you. And when they do, they'll generate all sorts of online buzz that will be indexed by the search engines, all relating to what your organization is up to. Forget about data-driven search engine technologies. The better approach to drive people to your stuff via the search engines is to create a World Wide Rave. As a result, your organization's web sites will quickly rise to prominence in the rankings on Google, Yahoo, and the other search engines.

That's it. Simple, right?

Sure, generating a World Wide Rave is as simple as can be. But again, when I discuss these ideas I find that they are so foreign to many people's thinking that they need much more than a list of rules in order to pull it off naturally. So the remainder of the book will be organized around these Rules of the Rave, so that you can learn them, too. My challenge to you is to implement them and create a World Wide Rave of your own.

TELLING STORIES

I often use the word *stories* when I talk about the content people want to share. I do that on purpose. People love to share stories. When someone says, "Let me tell you a story . . . ," you're interested, right? When someone says, "Let me tell you about my company's product . . . ," is your reaction the same? It doesn't sound like a way you want to spend your valuable time, does it? Stories are exciting. Most business writing is dry. That's why I've loaded these pages with 39 stories, most told directly by folks who created World Wide Raves. There will be how-to information, too, of course, but the reason I'm including so many stories in this book is that the fascinating people profiled here can explain, in their own words, their strategies for triggering a World Wide Rave much better than I can do with too many flowcharts, four-square diagrams, and to-do checklists. Stories sell.

So let's get moving. We'll start with one of my favorite stories about a World Wide Rave.

WHEN 7 = 350,000,000

Imagine you're the head of marketing at a theme park, and you're charged with announcing a major new attraction. What would you do?

Well, the old rules of marketing suggest that you pull out your wallet. You'd probably spend millions to buy your way into people's minds, interrupting them with TV spots, billboards by the side of the highway, and other "creative" Madison Avenue advertising techniques. You'd also hire a big PR agency, with staffers who would beg the media to write about your attraction. The traditional PR approach requires a self-congratulatory press release replete with company muckety-mucks claiming that the new attraction will bring about world peace by bringing families closer together.

That's not what Cindy Gordon, vice president, New Media Marketing at Universal Orlando Resort, did when she launched The Wizarding World of Harry Potter. Other large entertainment companies would have spent millions of dollars to interrupt everyone in the country with old-rules approaches: Super Bowl TV ads, blimps, direct mail, and magazine ads. Instead, Gordon told just seven people about the new attraction.

And those seven people told tens of thousands.

Then mainstream media listened to those tens of thousands and wrote about the news in their newspaper and magazine articles, in TV and radio reports, and in blog posts. Gordon estimates that 350 million people around the world heard the news that Universal Orlando Resort was creating The Wizarding World of Harry Potter theme park—all by telling just seven people.

TAPPING THE ENTHUSIASM OF MILLIONS OF FANS

Recognizing that millions of people around the world are passionate about all things Harry Potter, Gordon knew she could rely on a World Wide Rave to spread her story. After all, Harry is a global phenomenon. The series of books by author J.K. Rowling has been translated into 65 languages and has sold more than 325 million copies in more than 200 territories around the world. The films, produced by Warner Bros. Pictures, have grossed $3.5 billion worldwide at the box office alone.

Gordon and her counterpart at Warner Bros. chose to launch The Wizarding World of Harry Potter by first telling the exciting news to a very small group of rabid fans. Seven people at the top Harry Potter fan sites, such as Mugglenet,[1] were hand-selected by Gordon's team, with Warner Bros. and Rowling herself providing input about the choices. These seven (affectionately referred to by Gordon's team as "the AP of the HP world") were invited to participate in a top-secret webcast held at midnight on May 31, 2007.

The webcast was hosted by Scott Trowbridge, vice president of Universal Creative, and featured Stuart Craig, the Academy Award–winning production designer for all the Harry Potter films. In the webcast, live from the "Dumbledore's Office" set at Leavesden Studios, Craig discussed how his team of 20 designers is bringing together The Wizarding World of Harry Potter theme park.

[1] www.mugglenet.com/app/category/show/76

"If we hadn't gone to fans first, there could have been a backlash," Gordon says. She imagined the disappointment dedicated Harry Potter fans might feel if they learned about Universal Orlando's plans in, say, the *New York Times* rather than an insider fan site.

Soon after the webcast, the team sent an e-announcement to their in-house, opt-in email list of park guests so these consumers could hear the news directly, too. Team members also sent the e-announcement to friends and family. During the secret webcast, a Web microsite[2] went live to provide a place for bloggers and the media to link to for information on the theme park, which is slated to open in late 2009 or early 2010. Visitors to the site learned that the park will feature immersive rides and interactive attractions, as well as experiential shops and restaurants that will enable guests to sample fare from the wizarding world's best-known establishments.

Because Gordon's team launched The Wizarding World of Harry Potter through social media—putting fans first—they were able to run the entire promotion in-house, with a very small marketing budget (covering the webcast infrastructure and the microsite production) and a tiny development team. They did not hire an agency, and they did no widespread outbound media relations, no marketing stunts, no CEO conference calls, and no expensive advertising.

Of course, not all companies have Harry Potter on their team. But Gordon still accomplished a remarkable feat with an approach that most large organizations would not have taken. She told just seven people, and the power of the World Wide Rave she created led to 350 million people hearing the news.

Advice for generating a World Wide Rave

from Cindy Gordon, vice president of new media and marketing partnerships,
Universal Orlando Resort

"Nimble companies are using the Web in ways that they could never do before. New media has created a new marketing environment where the old rules of marketing no longer apply. When you have a passionate fan base for your brand, the Internet is especially vital. Communicating to a small but powerful group of fans first online to enlist their support is a smart way to ensure positive coverage in the mainstream press.

The power of the Internet makes it easier for people to fall in love with you faster. But beware—it also makes it easier for them to fall out of love with you faster. It's a double-edged sword. Listen constantly to what's being said about you. Social media technologies do not make a brand viral; they merely allow consumers to tell others about good brands.

The main thing is to be different and relevant with your brand. And when you have that, the sheer power of the Internet can accelerate your brand. Traditional media takes weeks to build brand awareness and months to build preference. The Internet can make your brand famous literally overnight."

. . . .

THE WORLD WIDE RAVE EMPOWERS YOU

The World Wide Rave is the single most empowering tool available to marketers today.

As you will learn, the formula for success includes a combination of some great—and free—Web content (a video, blog entry, interactive tool, or e-book) that provides valuable information (or is groundbreaking or amazing or hilarious or involves a celebrity), plus a network of people to light the fire and links that make your content very easy to share.

I wrote this book so you, too, can take advantage of the power of spreading ideas. These are the "new rules" that thousands of people have used to sell billions of dollars' worth of products and services worldwide.

 Success comes from self-publishing Web content that people want to share. It's not about gimmicks. It's not about paying an agency to interrupt others. It's about harnessing the World Wide Rave, the most powerful form of marketing there is.

Cindy Gordon of Universal Orlando Resort launched The Wizarding World of Harry Potter by publishing a microsite and a webcast. That's it. Using an idea-spreading strategy, she reached 350,000,000 people with two pieces of internally created Web content.

You can achieve similar success, and I'll show you how.

YOU MUST IGNORE THE OLD RULES OF ADVERTISING AND PR

It's worth saying one more time: A World Wide Rave is not about interruption. It's not about coercion, and it's not about buying access. Don't get sucked into gimmicks.

 In the old days, you either had to buy expensive advertising or beg the media to tell your story. Sadly, many organizations don't realize that they have a much better option—they can tell their story directly to an interested market.

The best World Wide Raves promote your organization and its products and services by delivering great online information tied directly to your products, services, and ideas (that's *tied to*, not *touting*). Success comes from the fact that people want to share this content with their friends, colleagues, and family members.

Since this isn't the same old advertising and PR that you and your agencies have been practicing for years, you'll need to throw out some old ideas and pick up some new ones:

> Don't obsess about being "on message."
>
> Don't beg mainstream media to write about you.
>
> Don't break the bank with expensive advertising.
>
> Do tell your story directly to an interested market.
>
> Do make it easy for people to share with others.

YOUR CHALLENGE: I've written this book to drive you to action. As you read it and learn from dozens of people who have achieved amazing success, your challenge is to ignore the advice of your agencies and instead think about what you can do to trigger a World Wide Rave of your own.

WE ARE THE WORLD

Obviously, ideas spread in many different ways long before we had the Web as a tool to tell our stories. Before the Web, ideas spread via word of mouth (the midnight ride of Paul Revere in April 1775 comes to mind) and via the mainstream media (television, radio, newspapers, and magazines). While this book is about spreading ideas *online*, it's worth looking at one offline World Wide Rave from the era before today's tools were available.

In 1985, in order to raise awareness of and encourage donations for famine-relief efforts in Ethiopia, a supergroup comprising 37 of the best-known artists of the day came together to record a charity single. "We Are the World" was written by Michael Jackson and Lionel Richie and produced and conducted by Quincy Jones. The recording session took place on January 28, 1985, immediately following the American Music Awards ceremony that evening. The single was released several months later and reached Number 1 on the U.S. Billboard Hot 100, remaining there for four weeks. It was the best-selling single in the United States. that year, and it reached Number 1 in other countries including the UK, Australia, Canada, and France. On April 5, 1985, a remarkable 8,000 radio stations around the world all played "We Are the World" at the same time. The World Wide Rave created by the song generated many millions of dollars for United Support of Artists for Africa Foundation (USA for Africa),[3] the charity created by the artists (who donated their time and services) to channel money to Africa.

While "We Are the World" was clearly a World Wide Rave, creating triggers for spreading ideas was much more difficult without the benefit of the Web. To create a World Wide Rave without the Internet required USA for Africa to overcome immense difficulties (e.g., wrangling the egos of dozens of the world's biggest pop stars). But you don't have Michael Jackson, Bruce Springsteen, and Stevie Wonder to help you spread your ideas. Thankfully, you don't need them.

A DREAM COME TRUE

As some of you may know, when I begin a presentation, I always ask a series of four questions and have the audience members raise their hands to answer "yes." Consider your own answers to these questions. In the past two months, either privately or professionally, in order to find an answer to a problem or research (or buy) a product, have you: (1) Responded to a direct-mail advertisement? (2) Used magazines, newspapers, TV, or radio? (3) Used Google or another search engine? (4) Emailed a friend, colleague, or family member (or used instant messaging, chat rooms, or equivalent) and received as a response a URL, which you then clicked to visit the web site? (Apologies to those of you who have answered these questions already.)

Over the course of a year, in front of more than 20,000 people from dozens of groups all over the world—including such diverse groups as

[3] www.usaforafrica.org/

college students, marketing professionals, and executives at Fortune 500 companies—the answers have been surprisingly consistent. Between 5 and 20 percent of people answer "yes" to the first two questions, which means that the ways that so many companies try to reach people today (direct mail, advertising, mainstream media) are effective in reaching only a small portion of potential customers. However, between 80 and 100 percent raise their hands for the last two questions. Clearly, providing great stuff on the Web is critical for any business.

Rather than trying to convince buyers to pay attention to your products and services by dreaming up messages and ad campaigns, offering great Web content delivers interested people right to your company's virtual doorstep. This is a marketer's dream come true!

FEAR NOT:
YOU, TOO, CAN CREATE A WORLD WIDE RAVE

Okay, can I guess what you were thinking after reading about Cindy Gordon and the World Wide Rave she created for The Wizarding World of Harry Potter? You might have muttered to yourself, "If I had access to J.K. Rowling and I was launching The Wizarding World of Harry Potter, I'd be able to think of something cool to do online, too. After all, there are millions of Harry Potter fans!" Sound about right? And maybe you also thought; "But I'm just a small-business person; what can I do?" (Or maybe you're a business-to-business marketer, or a real-estate agent, or the president of a university, or the singer in a rock band, or just about anyone.)

Fear not! The ideas in this book can help you reach your market, too.

YOUR CHALLENGE: Consider what's interesting about you and your organization. Why do people like to do business with you? How are you unique? Those are the things that you'll leverage to tell your story directly online and trigger a World Wide Rave.

I'll introduce you to many people just like you who have created their own World Wide Raves. Some, like Cindy Gordon, reached millions of people. However, others have generated online interest in smaller, yet no less important, ways. I've looked at hundreds and hundreds of examples of how ideas spread and why people tell stories on the Web, and in these pages I wanted to showcase examples that were as interesting and diverse as possible. Some organizations profiled here were already famous, but most were not. Some had marketing and promotional budgets at their disposal, but the majority just had some time and creativity to work with. Some were big, famous corporations, but others were small businesses, nonprofits, entrepreneurs, authors, and musicians. Here's a story of a woman who triggered a very different kind of World Wide Rave.

GIRLS FIGHT BACK!

Erin Weed, founder of Girls Fight Back!, uses her web site,[4] blog,[5] MySpace and Facebook groups, and YouTube videos[6] as a way to promote women's safety and self-defense issues. Weed started Girls Fight Back in 2001 in response to the tragic murder of Shannon McNamara, her friend and Alpha Phi sorority sister. Girls Fight Back makes safety education accessible, especially to young women in their teens and twenties, through

---

[4] www.girlsfightback.org
[5] www.erinweed.com/category/blog
[6] www.youtube.com/watch?v=uBLlqLb-DG4/

her educational web site and live seminars conducted all over the United States. She teaches girls and young women why they are their own best protectors, and then shows them how to reduce the risk of violence and fight back if necessary.

"Everything we do is about spreading the idea that girls can fight back," Weed says. "We need to give women the inspiration, confidence, and encouragement to fight back. If I had to choose, I'd say that confidence is the most important. So the community needs to come together to support giving women confidence."

All of the information on the site is free and available to girls all over the world. While the content helps to sell the live seminars Weed conducts at nearly 100 colleges, high schools, corporations, and community groups each year, she is thrilled to be helping many more people than will ever see her live presentations. "We get emails from people in places like Egypt who love the site because they have no ways to get the information in their own countries," she says. "So even in the places where we don't run seminars, we help empower people."

Weed is a big believer in using the Web, especially for her task of trying to teach young women about safety and self-defense. "There's a pretty huge stigma there, that women who know this stuff are man-haters and not femme at all," she says. "So we've been trying to make it cool to know how to stick up for yourself and fight back, which has been going very well. But I will say, the task would have been much more difficult without all the perks of the Net. This is a topic that women want to be well researched about before they take an actual class. People want to know, from the comfort of their own homes. We're talking about women's worst nightmares here, so this topic is really important to get out there and make it available for anyone to access free no matter where they are."

GET OUT YOUR MOBILE PHONES!

Anywhere from 200 to 1,000 people attend each hour-and-a-half-long seminar. "I'm always afraid that people will forget what they learned," Weed says. "I want the girls to remember the seminar later, and I want their friends to know what they've done when they get home."

Knowing her audience well has allowed Weed to create a terrific World Wide Rave trigger, a technique she uses at each of her live events. But it requires a setup. "When I am ready to speak in an auditorium with a thousand girls in the room, all one thousand always have their phones on," she says. "So, in the introduction I have the organizers tell people to turn the phones off." A collective sigh and slumping of shoulders follows.

Then, 90 minutes later, after a lively and fun interactive session at a high school or college, Weed asks the girls to take out their mobile phones. "At the very end of my presentation, I have them videotape a three-step self-defense series. They love it, and then they all post their homemade mobile-phone videos all over the Net, on Facebook and other places. It helps me to bond with the girls. They're like 'Wow, she's cool. She wants us to film.' And everyone is filming, with maybe 10 percent ending up on the Web. What better way to get them to remember what they learned than to put it onto the mobile phone and Facebook pages? They share it, too, so other girls who weren't there will see it."

Weed was also having a hard time getting the teen and college girls to log on to her web site after speaking gigs, and paper signup forms to gather email addresses for 500 or more girls at a time was impractical. "I realized we had to somehow get to them, as opposed to the other way around," she says. So, instead, I get all the girls to text message me their email addresses from their mobile phones, which automatically load to a web page." After the event, Weed sends personalized emails to each girl, customized for their school, inviting them to join the Girls Fight Back site to get access to other great resources. And get this: Nearly 100 percent of the girls volunteer their email addresses.

The concept of telling people that they aren't allowed to use mobile phones at the start of the session and then encouraging it later is brilliant. People like being a bit rebellious, doing things that they were told is not allowed. And many people like to share the experience with others, triggering a World Wide Rave.

Girls Fight Back has garnered significant attention from the mainstream press, with stories about Weed and her program appearing in newspapers (*The New York Times, The Washington Post,* more than 100 university publications), television *(CNN, Fox News)*, and magazines *(Cosmo Girl, Glamour, Marie Claire)*. The success of Girls Fight Back has helped Weed secure major corporate sponsors for her seminar tours. And her focus on creating valuable online information about self-protection (content that generates significant traffic from search engines), combined with the World Wide Rave of girls sharing mobile phone videos, is driving action. In October 2007, when Weed added new information to girlsfightback.org, traffic to the site doubled compared to the previous month and has continued to grow ever since. A testament to the search-engine-friendly content Weed publishes is that nearly half of the site's traffic comes from searches.

Advice for generating a World Wide Rave

from Erin Weed, founder of Girls Fight Back!

"You have to put your information out there so people see it and know that you're full of great ideas. But business owners are living in fear of having their content stolen on the Web, so they don't put it up. I think as people who are living in a world where we have information to share that can improve people's lives, we need to share. When you share what you know, people will be helped, and that will ultimately come back to you in the form of recognition and business. Why wouldn't I share with someone how to palm-strike an attacker in the face when that could clearly save a girl's life?"

. . . .

YOUR CHALLENGE: What slightly subversive (but not illegal or unethical) strategies, like encouraging people to use their mobile phones in a place where it is not normally allowed, can you use to trigger a World Wide Rave?

NOBODY CARES ABOUT YOUR PRODUCTS

ABOUT YOUR

PRODUCTS

(Except You)

UNDERSTAND BUYER PERSONAS TO TRIGGER A WORLD WIDE RAVE

Buyer personas are one of the most fundamental aspects of great marketing. A *buyer persona* represents a distinct group of potential customers, or an archetypal person whom you want your marketing to reach. Targeting your work to buyer personas prevents you from sitting on your butt in your comfortable office just making stuff up about your products, which is the cause of most ineffective marketing.

Incidentally, my use of the word *buyer* applies to any organization's target customers. A politician's buyer personas include voters, supporters, and contributors; universities' buyer personas include prospective students and their parents; a tennis club's buyer personas are potential members; and nonprofits' buyer personas include corporate and individual donors. Go ahead and substitute however you refer to your potential customers in the phrase *buyer persona,* but do keep your focus on this concept. It is critical for success online.

 By truly understanding the market problems that your products and services solve for your buyer personas, you transform your marketing from mere product-specific, egocentric gobbledygook that only you understand and care about into valuable information people are eager to consume and that they use to make the choice to do business with your organization.

Instead of creating jargon-filled, hype-based advertising, you can create the kind of online information that your buyers naturally gravitate to—if you take the time to listen to them discuss the problems that you can help them solve. Then you'll be able to use *their* words, *not* your own. You'll speak in the language of your buyer, not the language of your founder, CEO, product manager, or PR agency staffer. You'll help your marketing get real.

I LOVE A GOOD AUDIT

What would you do if you were a marketing executive at a software company that sells products for internal auditors and controllers at large corporations? Assume your company is an independent, competing with the big boys whose greater name recognition threatens your ability to get noticed in the enterprise software business? If you're like most marketers in such companies, you try to talk about how your products are better than the other guys'. You develop jargon-laden product messaging about your "flexible, scalable solutions" that are built with "cutting-edge technology" and serve a "mission-critical application" within your "top worldwide clients." (Yes, this really is the sort of crap many companies churn out. If you're at all familiar with the enterprise software market, you've no doubt read pages of this worthless copy.) But this nonsense just doesn't resonate with buyers. When everyone uses the same language and all companies obsess over technical minutiae of how their products are superior, customers can't make any sense of who's got what. As a result, buyers tend to go with the "safe alternative"—the big famous players in the market.

Michael Evans, vice president of marketing for enterprise software provider Approva,[7] doesn't use the same old sales and marketing playbook. Instead he focuses his company's efforts on a much better way of competing: building a marketing strategy that communicates directly with his buyer personas—treating them like real people and talking to them in the context of their own needs.

[7] www.approva.net/

Approva's products are used by Fortune 500–sized companies to identify and prevent fraud. Well-known software giants like Oracle and SAP also sell similar products, but they use the same-old marketing strategies we discussed earlier.

"We noticed that the Information Technology groups within our potential customers are being marketed everything," Evans says. "But the internal audit department and the controllers' office is not overmarketed to, so we chose to communicate directly to them—the people who will actually benefit from our products. When they see something that is interesting, they are much more likely to respond."

Evans created fun communications with an auditor-friendly theme to appeal directly to his buyer personas.

"At first, we handed out buttons that said 'I Love a Good Audit' at tradeshows such as the Institute of Internal Auditors. When people saw the buttons, they got excited and really wanted one. Many people came to the booth and asked for multiple buttons, and some were specific, saying things like 'I need two buttons, one for my CFO and one for my CEO.' Because it was fun, people were receptive to hearing what we do."

Expanding on the popularity of the buttons, Evans and his team created a microsite[8] where people could "Tell us about the first time you fell in love with your audit," send e-cards to their friends and colleagues, and deliver unexpected love messages to fellow auditors in a virtual-refrigerator-magnet format. "The challenge for us is that internal audit is not an exciting topic," he says. "So we wanted to have some fun without being serious."

[8] www.iloveagoodaudit.com/

A company blog called *Audit Trail* was then developed and used as a tool to communicate both serious information as well as the more off-beat material that buyer personas really enjoy and that Approva was becoming famous for. A particular hit was a video the company created to wish the Sarbanes-Oxley Act (SOX) a happy fifth birthday. SOX is a federal law enacted in response to corporate accounting scandals at companies like Enron, Tyco International, and WorldCom. It established new or enhanced standards for all U.S. public companies. While many developers besides Approva sell software to help big companies manage SOX compliance, nearly all of them focus on the dreadfully boring aspects of what the products actually do.

The music video exclusive *Happy 5th Birthday Sarbanes-Oxley*[9] features Steven Zelin, The Singing CPA,[10] and was passed around by many potential Approva customers around the time of the "birthday." The video became a World Wide Rave as many people blogged about the video and shared it via email. Accountants live and breathe the complicated policies of Sarbanes-Oxley every day, so the light-hearted and surprising video was appreciated by these hard workers. Some left comments on the Approva *Audit Trail* blog. For example, David wrote, "Funny and catchy way to celebrate the biggest buzz in accounting in some time." Harry Dery wrote, "I'm sending this link to everyone I know who has ever had a complaint about [SOX]—which is everyone!" DW wrote, ". . . it truly takes a special talent to be able to fit the words 'corporate malfeasance' into such a witty ditty."

Can you imagine such expressions of goodwill and interest showing up on a site full of traditional product-centric marketing gibberish? Of course not. And Evans believes the positive customer contact pays serious dividends.

[9] www.approva.net/audittrail/2007/07/12/happy-fifth-birthday-sarbanes-oxley-music-video/
[10] www.stevenzelin.com/

"This type of marketing enhances our brand by conveying that we're a fun company to work with and helps keep a prospect warm, engaged, and responsive even when they may still be a couple of months away from an active buying cycle," Evans says. "We're stunned by our own success. Within the first six months, the blog overtook the number of visitors to the company web site. Now people in the industry know who we are, because we've accurately communicated the culture of the company externally. Now when employees talk about the company, they use words like 'we're fun and creative.' Our customers *like* to work with us."

What makes the Approva approach work so well is the absolute focus on their important buyer persona: internal auditors at Fortune 500 companies. When you focus on your buyers, you're taking the first, and most important, step to triggering a World Wide Rave.

YOUR CHALLENGE: Get out of your nice comfortable office and speak with members of your buyer personas. Meet them on their own turf—their home, office, or where they go for fun—and listen to their problems. Then create something interesting and valuable especially for them, and offer it for free on the Web.

Sometimes, when I first introduce the concept of buyer personas, people are (quite naturally) a little wary. They don't immediately see the value and often fall back on the tried-and-true methods, blabbing on and on about what their damn products do (instead of what problems they solve for their buyers). I usually find in these cases that it's extremely helpful to discuss another example, one from a completely different industry's buyer persona, and how a real organization solved problems for that group. So let's do that, shall we?

STUPID CANCER:
I'M TOO YOUNG FOR THIS!

As a young cancer patient and then cancer survivor, Matthew Zachary was incensed by the huge cancer information and awareness gap affecting young adults. Every cancer support group he encountered focused on young children or older adults. When he realized there was a buyer persona that was ignored by the big cancer groups such as the National Cancer Society, he decided to close the information gap by founding I'm Too Young For This![11] (abbreviated "i[2]y"), a pioneering, survivor-led cancer foundation dedicated to advocacy, support, and research exclusively on behalf of survivors and care providers under the age of 40.

Zachary has built i[2]y into a World Wide Rave by focusing virtually all of his efforts toward online advocacy. "Everything we've done has been completely through the Web, and it has become a global phenomenon," Zachary says. "We don't do any major outreach, we don't have any PR plan. It was a perfect storm of putting something consumer-friendly around a cause that nobody knew existed [within] the spectrum of cancer, which everyone knows about."

The terrific i[2]y site, a *TIME Magazine* Best 50 Website, serves as the centralized location for young adults to learn about cancer. "We engage young people through innovations in social media," Zachary says. "It's the evolution of clicks-and-mortar around user-generated content and patient-centered healthcare."

Zachary says he and i[2]y are at the forefront of what he calls "health 2.0" (Web-based healthcare). His expertise is in demand, and he sits on

[11] http://i2y.org

the advisory board of Google for healthcare issues, is frequently quoted in the press, and appears on TV to speak about reaching young people who have health issues. "We're using music, the arts, and social media to organize, mobilize, and activate young adults to the cause; to destigmatize cancer as a death sentence; and to make it hip to talk openly about stupid cancer," he says.

There are a million cancer survivors under 40 in the United States today, and until i[2]y came along, they had nowhere to turn. "If you're nineteen years old and you have breast cancer, you're lumped into a group with grannies," Zachary says. "We want people to feel special and want patients and survivors who are in their twenties and thirties to know that they are part of an exclusive global community. We use social networking and viral marketing to touch a nerve. . . .We're the Howard Stern of cancer. I have a live webcast called the Stupid Cancer Show with thousands of listeners, and the Stupid Cancer Blog[12] is syndicated through Steve Case's Revolution Health. The site and blog are linked to from more than 500 blogs, and there is a sphere of influence, through Facebook and other places, of tens of thousands of people. We're exploiting YouTube and Digg as other ways to reach our market."

The i[2]y organization is all-digital, with the lone exception being literature for young people that is available in 390 cancer centers. "The flyer is simple," Zachary says. "'Cancer sucks if you're under forty. No one cares. But we do. So go to our site.' It's all about disruption and the youth culture and getting people online. So we use the tools of the 'me generation' to get the interest of young people in the issues that they care about."

---

[12] http://imtooyoungforthis.blogspot.com/

Advice for generating a World Wide Rave

from Matthew Zachary, founder and executive director, I'm Too Young For This!

"We've gotten noticed because we're ageist, not diseasist. We are the only people talking about cancer for young people. Everyone else talks about a particular kind of cancer. Bald, dying kids don't sell to young people. It doesn't matter if it's cancer, cleft palate, or other issues: Guilt may work for boomers and seniors, but the youth market is too narcissistic to care. Know your audience and be crystal clear and transparent."

•••••••••••••••••••••

FORGET ABOUT YOUR PRODUCTS

Let's take a hint from Zachary and be honest for a second, okay?

Nobody cares about your products and services except you and the others in your organization.

What your personas *do* care about is themselves. And they care a great deal about solving their problems. The good news for you smart marketers who get *Tuned In* to buyer personas (which I've written about in my previous books) is that this knowledge has the potential to make you many times more successful. It may quite literally transform your business (that's not just my opinion; many people write in to tell me so).

When it's obvious that you understand your buyers and their problems, it jars your visitors into paying attention. The result is a World Wide Rave of people who are excited that your organization might be able to help them.

Companies that understand their buyer personas know *exactly* why people will be eager to learn about their products and services. These organizations get out of Sales Mode and instead work to educate potential buyers. That's why this concept of buyer personas is so critically important for all forms of marketing—it's also why I write about it a lot. But it's especially important for triggering a World Wide Rave. A focus on buyer personas transforms your marketing (and your business). Really.

Liam Ovenden, founder and managing director of Sydney, Australia–based RPO Group,[13] a human resources recruitment outsourcing company, is an entrepreneur who develops online content for the right reasons, *not* to satisfy his own ego and *not* to prattle on about what his products do. "People come to RPO Group because of high employee turnover, missed headcount targets, and an inability to hire people in volume," says Ovenden. "We get them the people they need, in the numbers they need, at the time they need to fulfill their business plans at an efficient cost." When I spoke with Ovenden, he was reluctant to talk about his products and services at all. He simply told me, "We handle recruitment, so that you can get on with your business."

When I pressed again, Ovenden said, "Our company embeds staffing functions inside organizations and runs them on their behalf. The technical term for it is Recruitment Process Outsourcing (RPO). Hence our name, RPO Group." Okay—this gobbledygook-laden phrase is the way that most companies speak. Note that Ovenden was reluctant to use this corporate-type language until I pressed him. And it should go without saying that this jargon-filled approach is much less effective than talking like a human is.

Now, if you're familiar with traditional business-school-style marketing that stresses the *P*s (typically the four *P*s are identified as Product, Pricing, Promotion, and Placement, although some say there are five or six *P*s, including others like Packaging and Publicity), and you were charged with developing a marketing plan for RPO Group, you'd no doubt create a bunch of "product messages" about RPO products and services, throwing around phrases like "Recruitment Process Outsourcing." But this approach is doomed to fail on the Web. Why? Because nobody cares about Recruitment Process Outsourcing, except Recruitment Process Outsourcing companies, of course. Mumbo-jumbo about your products won't appeal to your buyer personas, because they simply don't care about you, your company, and what you do.

RPO Group's clients range from Fortune 500 names like Verizon to global businesses like Colliers International and fast-growing entrepreneurial companies like the BCI Group. Typically, RPO Group assumes the entire recruitment load for its clients, hiring administrative, technical, professional, and executive-level positions.

The buyer personas Ovenden targets include chief executive officers, chief financial officers, and chief operating officers (CEOs, CFOs, and COOs, respectively, aka "C-level executives").

"Our buyer personas are not subject-matter experts in what we do," Ovenden says. "'Talent' is important to them, but 'recruitment' is not. Since our buyers are not subject-matter experts, we create everything in plain English, relating to everyday situations, so that we are easily understood. We also try to make the direct link between household company names that everyone equates with sustained success and the ingrained culture and history they have of out-recruiting their competition."

Ovenden and his team developed buyer persona profiles for each of the C-level buyers they target. To make the buyer profiles come alive, he named each one and included a representative photograph. For example, "Rick Johnson" is "CEO of a medium-to-large Australian organization or the subsidiary of an international organization" and is the composite of all of the CEOs that Ovenden and his team worked with. Ovenden's team wrote several pages of details on the "Rick Johnson" buyer persona, gathered by interviewing actual CEOs. This process helped the buyer persona come alive for RPO Group. Of course, buyer persona profiles like those created at RPO Group are for *internal use only* and are never shared on your site.

It's important to build personas based on your ideal buyers, not based on your existing customers. Most organizations' current customers represent just a small fraction of the potential market compared to potential customers, so when you develop buyer personas, you should be thinking of the vast untapped market potential rather than the people you currently serve. And you should develop a composite buyer persona based on interviewing a dozen or more people rather than relying on one person. For that reason, it is best to use ideal buyer personas (like RPO Group's "Rick Johnson") rather than a real customer that your company currently serves.

When you truly know your buyer personas, you're ready to transform your marketing and generate a World Wide Rave.

Unlike the vast majority of company web sites, which are nothing more than egotistical, product-oriented nonsense, the RPO Group web site is written from the various buyer personas' perspectives. It uses the words and phrases executives use to describe the problems they face—and RPO Group solves. Here's a sample (note how these are not product statements, which is typical of most sites, but instead focus on the problems faced by buyers):

If you are experiencing some or all of these symptoms, and want to do something about it, then contact us:

- Service to customers impacted by staff turnover
- Sales targets missed through key defections
- Staff morale low
- Poor internal succession planning
- Recruitment costs high, for questionable outcomes
- Lack of data, metrics, analysis, or insight into how effectively you recruit, retain, and redeploy your talent
- Unable to budget and plan for headcount and performance targets with confidence

ARE YOU A TALENT FANATIC?

RPO Group's Web initiatives include much more than just a web site. "Our belief in the logic and efficacy of the new rules of marketing and PR led us to immediately change direction and reengineer the way we attract customers with a new web site (content-rich, of course!); a personal blog *(The Talent Fanatic)*; and useful, web-ready content," Ovenden says. "Oh, we also let go our PR agency. Although they were great people and good [at what they did], they were following the 'old rules.'"

Ovenden writes *The Talent Fanatic* blog himself. Unlike many other companies, which create only a basic link to theirs (e.g., "Click here for our blog"), RPO Group designed the blog link on its homepage to appeal directly to buyer personas with links such as "Are you a Talent Fanatic?" and "Why does talent matter and how do you get your unfair share of it?"

In addition, Ovenden and his team published a free e-book called *5 Secrets of Talent: What the world's best organizations don't want you to know about recruitment & talent management.*[14] Because Ovenden started with his buyer personas in mind, the title and content were written using the language of his potential customers. "We stayed away from the term *recruitment* and instead used the more generic term *talent*," he says. "Our intended audience—C-level executives who are decision-makers, not recruiters—would tend to see recruitment as tactical and technical and not of particular interest to them, whereas talent is strategic and does impact them and is something they want to know more about. I really have one aim in writing it—to change the mindset of C-level executives toward recruitment. I hope it gives some insight into the central importance of doing it well and opens their eyes to the enormous opportunities for them in being the best recruiting organization they can be. We tried to make the 5 *Secrets* practical initiatives that these people can make a decision to implement and that will have a hugely positive impact on their company."

Ovenden says it was a leap of faith to change the way RPO Group marketed the company. "It instinctively appealed to us to give away great content in the belief that customers will want to know more and come back to us," he says. "Our online marketing and PR strategy is targeted at getting our thoughts and tools into the hands of those who are searching for answers on the Web. We've got a web site that lives, is dynamic, is full of information and insight written in plain English—a resource for a C-level executive to come to get bite-sized pieces of usable information that can be implemented in their business. But most importantly, now we've got qualified buyers coming to our web site and being turned from strangers into friends. And that makes our business development infinitely more successful, which was the whole point in the first place. So far, all I can report is great news."

Advice for generating a World Wide Rave

from Liam Ovenden, founder and managing director of RPO Group

"Professional services firms are uniquely suited to creating great online content, because our ideas are what we trade on. The leap of faith is to 'give away for free' that which you usually charge for in the hope it comes back to you in people wanting you to help them do it properly."

● ●

YOUR CHALLENGE: Never talk about your products and services again. Instead, focus on your buyer personas and how you can solve problems for them.

HOW BIG IS YOUR "WORLD"?

Let's pause for just a moment and talk about the size of your world. When I use the phrase *World Wide Rave*, people often think that the ideas in this book matter only to organizations capable of reaching millions of readers, viewers, or listeners via a global phenomenon. As a result, some people just aren't interested in trying to create a World Wide Rave because they don't have a huge potential market. They think these ideas are not for them.

Fear not!

A World Wide Rave is about reaching your buyer personas—the people who will be interested in your products and services. For you, that might be a market of just ten people—or ten million. No matter the size of your market, when people are spreading your ideas online, it's the best endorsement possible and a proven path to increased sales, fame, and fortune.

Sure, Cindy Gordon (whom we met at the beginning of this book) has a potential market in the hundreds of millions, because that happens to be the number of people who enjoy the Harry Potter books and movies and might want to visit The Wizarding World of Harry Potter theme park. In Gordon's case, we'd be right to define a World Wide Rave as reaching hundereds of millions of people online. By that standard, she was successful.

However, most organizations have significantly smaller target markets or sell only to people in a small geographical area. For example, if you're selling to C-level executives at larger companies in the Asia-Pacific region (like Liam Ovenden at RPO Group does), your market is much smaller than Cindy Gordon's. But you can still trigger a World Wide Rave. If several thousand Asia-Pacific-based C-level executives read Ovenden's e-book and blog, the percentage of his market exposed to the RPO Group's ideas could match Gordon's percentage, which required tens of millions for The Wizarding World of Harry Potter. My point here is that RPO Group achieved a World Wide Rave within the sphere of their buyer personas, just like Universal Orlando Resorts did with theirs. It's just that the "world" for RPO Group is a tiny fraction of the size of Planet Harry Potter.

If you run a church in Boston, for you a World Wide Rave might be reaching everyone in the Boston area looking for a new church—that would be a small number of people living in the "world" of Metro Boston. Similarly, Cervelo Cycles sells expensive racing bikes for road racers and triathletes. Since the market for a bicycle that sells for $5,000 or more is small (but includes customers from all over the world), so will the community consuming Cervelo Cycles'[15] terrific on-line information be small, yet global. A World Wide Rave for Cervelo Cycles is just as important, because it means their buyer personas are talking about them. That buzz is what sells their products.

A RESUME? OR AN E-BOOK?

I've got another hypothetical situation for you to illustrate the point that people care about their problems, not your product. This time, the product is a person.

What would you do if you were a vice president of marketing for a technology company and you were ready to find a new opportunity to advance your career? Well, if you're like virtually every other job seeker, you'd prepare a resume, obsessing over every entry to make sure it paints your background in the best possible light. You'd also begin a networking campaign, emailing and phoning your contacts and using social networking tools like LinkedIn, hoping that someone in your extended network knows of a suitable job opportunity.

Basically, the old rules of job searches required you to interrupt people to tell them that you were on the market and to beg them to help you. The approach is just like traditional product-centric advertising, with your resume serving as a product brochure for the product: you.

[15] www.cervelo.com/

Steve Chazin is not a typical job seeker.

Instead of following the traditional path, in September 2007, Chazin started a blog[16] and wrote an e-book, *Marketing Apple: 5 Secrets of the World's Best Marketing Machine*,[17] which he offered online for free.

Then Chazin waited for the world to find him.

He didn't have to wait long; the first day saw 2,900 downloads of *Marketing Apple*, with 2,100 on the second day and an average of 300 per day in the three months that followed. In a very short time, tens of thousands of people downloaded *Marketing Apple*, and hundreds of people wrote about it on their blogs. Chazin propelled himself into the world as a recognized expert on the kind of marketing used by Apple, Inc. And he instantly set himself far apart from the rest of the pack of job seekers looking for consulting work or VP of marketing jobs.

Chazin had spent nearly a decade at Apple, where he managed a New England sales territory, drove a strategic partnership with the Harvard Business School, and worked with Steve Jobs to rebuild Apple's marketing efforts. His efforts helped return the company to profitability in the late 1990s. Thus, Chazin understands how Apple markets products, and he offers insider advice in his e-book and on his blog. His five secrets, which should be both interesting to and relevant for all marketing professionals, are neatly packaged to make it easy to learn how Apple operates. Chazin's MarketingApple.com is open to anyone who wants to learn and implement some of the techniques that have made Apple, Inc. the world's best marketing machine.

"Apple is a perfect example of what good design and good marketing can do when you tie them both together," Chazin says. "My background

[16] www.MarketingApple.com/
[17] www.marketingapple.com/Marketing_Apple_e-book.pdf

and my love for the company put me in a unique position to help others embrace a similar approach. And I help fellow marketers look good!"

The exposure that the e-book and blog have given Chazin mean he's become a go-to source for reporters looking for insight into Apple's marketing; he's been interviewed by several major publications, including the *Los Angeles Times.* Just a month after releasing the e-book, he was invited to Kiev, Ukraine, to deliver a (paid) speech about how better marketing saved Apple from extinction. Since then, he's been offered additional invitations to speak in other locations.

"I've got a traditional resume, but it doesn't tell people how I think," Chazin says. "They get a sense of who I am from the e-book and the blog in a way that a resume can't possibly deliver. There is also a sense of importance that the e-book has that a resume doesn't. The e-book is free, but it has a very real perceived value."

Chazin's job-search strategy definitely paid off. He says the blog and e-book have helped him put out a virtual shingle, landing him the consulting work he was seeking. "It has raised my profile significantly," he says. "I've gotten unsolicited emails from people who want my advice and help, and that's led to several consulting deals. Funny enough, it has also given me more notoriety at Apple, and it reconnected me to some of my old colleagues. I'm told that many people at Apple read my blog."

The effects of *Marketing Apple* and Chazin's World Wide Rave effort sure beat being viewed as one resume out of thousands. And it worked because he created buzz by helping potential buyers (employers and those hiring him to work on projects) solve their problems.

Advice for generating a World Wide Rave

from Steve Chazin, author of *Marketing Apple*

"One of my simple marketing rules found in the *Marketing Apple* e-book is 'Make Your Message Memorable.' Simply put, you have little chance that something will go viral unless, like a disease, it can be spread easily mouth-to-mouth. For that to happen, your message has to be supertight and easy to transmit in as few words as possible. '1,000 songs in your pocket' is the answer to 'What is an iPod?' Before that, the Macintosh was introduced as 'The computer for the rest of us.' If you can boil your message down to just its syrupy goodness, you can achieve lift—the irresistible force of millions of customers selling your product for you."

. . . .

The e-book is one of the most powerful forms of Web content and has particularly strong potential to trigger a World Wide Rave. Steve Chazin found incredible success with this medium. And the first time I told his story was in my own free e-book, *The New Rules of Viral Marketing,*[18] which was downloaded more than 100,000 times in just the first three months it was available. In fact, e-books are becoming such a valuable marketing tool that it's worth looking at some other examples from very different markets.

[18] www.davidmeermanscott.com/documents/Viral_Marketing.pdf

WHAT ABOUT
BUSINESS-TO-BUSINESS E-BOOKS?

Part of why e-books have become such a significant medium to generate a World Wide Rave is that people can instantly see the value of a product that looks like for-purchase content but can actually be downloaded for free. In my opinion, e-books should be material people *want* to read, as opposed to the dense and usually boring whitepapers, which are full of product-centric content and which our buyers feel they *should* read but often don't.

For business-to-business companies used to the more traditional whitepaper, an e-book is a radical departure for one simple, yet revolutionary reason: its goal. For most companies, a whitepaper is about generating sales leads. An e-book, however, is about spreading ideas. Improved sales are a byproduct, though obviously an important one.

If you've already created and published a whitepaper for your business, it's highly likely that you built in all sorts of controls over its dissemination. If you offered it online, you probably required readers to fill out a Web form before they could download it. The form required them to supply their name, affiliation, email address, phone number, and perhaps details like the size of their company. Most companies apply the same "give-to-get" philosophy to offline whitepapers, requiring interested readers to supply a business card or fill out a reply form.

An e-book is different, or at least should be. Make the content totally free, with no registration requirement at all, so people are more likely to download it and share with colleagues. For example, an e-book called *The Taxonomy Folksonomy Cookbook: Finding the Right Recipe for Organizing Enterprise Metadata*[19] from Dow Jones Client Solutions was written for information professionals. It exemplifies a creative way to communicate about complicated ideas like information tagging and metadata use in large organizations. The e-book has been very popular with the *corporate librarian* buyer persona, a major target market for Dow Jones Client Solutions. Librarians find the e-book through partner links on association sites, such as the Special Libraries Association, and events such as the Semantic Technology Conference, Taxonomy Boot Camp, Enterprise Search Summit, and KM World. Attendees at these conferences can spend the following year removing themselves from the mailing lists they're forced onto by signing up to get free information. Imagine what a refreshing change of pace it is to be able to examine the content first and then decide to opt into a mailing list for more information later.

[19] http://solutions.dowjones.com/taxonomyebook

HOW TO MAKE YOUR E-BOOK A WORLD WIDE RAVE

Are you wondering how to pull all that off? Here are some tips for executing a successful e-book:

- Study e-books such as my *The New Rules of Viral Marketing* and Chazin's *Marketing Apple* to learn how to put one together.

- Write the e-book to address a problem your buyer persona faces. Don't write about your products and services.

- Present your e-book in a landscape format, rather than the whitepaper's typical portrait format. This design choice signals to your readers that the content inside is *interesting*, since it looks different from a boring old whitepaper. And because it fits perfectly in a computer screen, it also indicates you should read it *now*, online, instead of printing it out for later.

- E-books can be as short as 10 or 12 pages or as long as 50 to 60 pages. Because you use graphics and whitespace, this translates to about 5 to 25 pages of text. If you have more than 30 pages, consider breaking the content up into several e-books and releasing them as a series.

- Include attractive graphics and images with the text.

- Consider writing in a lighter, more conversational style than you would in a whitepaper, marketing brochure, or Web page.

- E-books (as World Wide Rave marketing tools) should always be free and should *never* have a registration requirement.

- Think like a publisher by understanding your audience. Consider what market problems your audience has, and develop a topic that appeals to these readers.

- Try to make the e-book easy to read. Keep things fun and exciting.

- Open with a story. Use examples and stories throughout.

- Consider how you can include conflict in your writing to make it snappy and keep the reader's interest.

- Find a great title that grabs the reader's attention. Use a subtitle to describe what the e-book will deliver.

- Hire a professional editor to help you through multiple drafts and a proofreader to finalize the copy.

- Have the e-book professionally designed.

- Put a Creative Commons license[20] on the content so people know they can freely share your copyrighted material.

- Create a landing page from which people can download your e-book. For an example, check out the Pragmatic Marketing, Inc. e-book *The Secrets of Tuned In Leaders: How technology company CEOs create success (and why most fail).*[21]

- Promote the e-book like crazy. Offer it on your web site with easy-to-find links. If you have a blog, write about it there. Add a link to your employees' e-mail signatures. Get partners to offer links.

- To drive the World Wide Rave, alert bloggers, analysts, and members of the mainstream media that the e-book is available, and send them a download link. Don't send the actual PDF document directly unless asked.

---

[20] http://creativecommons.org/
[21] www.pragmaticmarketing.com/secrets

SEX, SHAVING, AND YOUR ORAL HEALTH

Two e-books released in 2008 suggest that virtually any product or service can benefit from the exposure in an e-book that has the potential to become a World Wide Rave, and both of them involve sex. Sort of.

An e-book called *The 6 Essential Elements to an Exceptional Shave!*[22] asks: "Were you taught how to shave by a pro? More likely you've unknowingly taken on the bad habits of your father, or even worse, you've taught yourself to shave from what you've seen on television commercials. If you ever get razor burn, ingrown hairs, redness or irritation then you have to read on!"

Released by VitaMan, an Australian company that sells men's shaving, skin, and hair grooming products to the retail and professional market, the e-book includes six reasons why you should pay attention to your daily routine. The final one really captures readers' attention: "The amount of sex you get is in direct proportion to how well you shave!"

Dr. Helaine Smith, a Boston cosmetic dentist who focuses on smile makeovers and how they help improve people's lives, takes a similar e-book approach. She first asks the question: "When was the last time you thought about your teeth? That's like asking when you last thought about your femur or your elbow."

In her e-book, *Healthy Mouth, Healthy Sex!*,[23] Dr. Smith goes on to explain the connection between oral health and sexual well-being, "a topic not too many people talk about." She says: "What many people don't understand—or even consider—is that the health of our teeth and mouths has a huge connection with our overall physical health—and our sex lives!"

[22] www.vitamanglobal.com/exceptional-shave/
[23] http://helainesmithdmd.blogspot.com/2008/03/healthy-mouth-healthy-sex-free-e-book.html

I really like these e-books. The sex angle, while pushing the envelope just a teeny bit, does spark some interest because the authors are linking sex to unexpected things like shaving and dentistry. And if a Massachusetts cosmetic dentist and an Australian company that produces "male grooming products that were created to increase the appeal of the uncompromising man" can find topics to write an e-book about, it shows that virtually any company, person, or organization can use an e-book to tell a story. You can, too.

E-BOOK YOUR WAY
TO FAME AND FORTUNE

This is a new world for marketers and corporate communicators. Never before has a medium allowed an idea (or a product) to spread instantly to millions of consumers. E-books are true examples of thought leadership at work, and they hold the potential to influence many thousands of people in ways that traditional marketing cannot.

YOUR CHALLENGE: E-books are a great way to dip your toes into the ocean of the World Wide Rave. If you're a thought leader—a person recognized as having innovative and important ideas—go ahead and write an e-book. I dare you. (And if you do, please send me the link!)

YOU CAN'T DO THAT WITH THE YELLOW PAGES

Dr. Smith did more than just author *Healthy Mouth, Healthy Sex!* She turned herself into a one-woman online marketing machine. She's maintained a content-rich web site[24] for years and recently added a blog and a podcast. "I've spent so much money over the years on marketing," Smith says. "I even started a group of eight cosmetic dentists to do radio ads for $80,000. But not one of us got any results from that effort. I placed advertising in *Boston* magazine, and it was a waste of money. And I was always aggressive with Yellow Page advertising—for example, I had a huge two-page ad in the Yellow Pages, paying $2,000 a month. Today we get so much business from the Internet, we don't need anything else. When the web site became successful, I decided to stop buying Yellow Page ads, and when I told the Yellow Page salesman, he got really angry and said, 'What if you fail!' But I didn't fail, and I haven't done any Yellow Page ads in six years!"

Smith's practice focuses on new dentistry techniques, and she spends time researching new methods and ideas with the goal of quickly implementing them in her work. "Everything I do, particularly the dentistry, is new. So I wanted my marketing to be the same. I jumped into the world of blogging, podcasting, and other ways of generating interest in what I do." Because she runs a business and spends a great deal of time with patients, Smith works with Dianna Huff of DH Communications, Inc.,[25] who helps her implement her ideas quickly.

Smith was eager to create an e-book, but she needed a great topic. "One day I had *The Today Show* on television and they were talking about sex.

[24] www.helainesmithdmd.com/
[25] www.dhcommunications.com/

I'd recently become incensed about the link between oral sex and disease, so right after that I did a press release about braces ripping condoms. It was amazing, because I had reporters calling me and my web site traffic went way up, so that's when I began forming the idea of wanting to talk more about the idea. Soon after, I had a gynecologist in for a cleaning, and we agreed that the topic was needed but I knew that just talking to the *Boston Globe* would not do the trick. So the e-book seemed like the best approach."

Interestingly, Smith found that most dentists opposed talking about the link between oral sex and disease. "The American Dental Association would not appreciate this because they are so conservative, so I did not even send it to them," she says. "I've had no negative reaction from other dentists once it came out."

Smith's World Wide Rave has not only transformed her business, it has also allowed her to focus on showcasing her personality to potential clients in ways that are impossible offline. "It's been amazing," she says. "Even though I am a direct and opinioned person, I am also a quiet person. By creating all of this valuable information online, I am able to be who I really am. My site, blog, and e-book scream to people before they meet me. So the people who reach out to me already know who I am, and therefore people are more willing to choose to work with me. You can't do any of that with the old ways. Even a TV campaign cannot get that information out."

Smith asks new patients how they heard of her and keeps track of the statistics. "From the Web content alone there is between $10,000 and $15,000 a month in new business, and I consistently get around twelve to fifteen new patients each month via the Web. And what's remarkable is that it is consistent month-to-month. The new business keeps coming in." Smith has so much business coming her way, that in just a few years she has gone from 2 employees to 14.

Advice for generating a World Wide Rave

from Dr. Helaine Smith, author of *Healthy Mouth, Healthy Sex!*

"My core competence is cosmetic dentistry. Even though I have enthusiasm and creativity when it comes to marketing, and I blog, I need to have experts who can help with things like writing and search engine optimization.

I suggest finding people who really know what they are doing and bring them onto your team. As entrepreneurs, dentists are required to do everything, from sitting with patients, to sending bills, to cleaning the bathrooms. We're on our own. But believe me, if I can do this kind of marketing, anyone can."

. . . .

WHEN NOT TO HAVE SEX
(in your e-book)

And while we're on the subject of sex, we all need to be sure when we do associate with something provocative, or with a significant news story that people might search for online, that the association is legitimate. Our use of the provocative or newsworthy term must hold up in people's minds. For instance, a random association to Britney Spears just to drive traffic from people looking for information on the pop tart is not okay because it is a bait-and-switch. However, the sex angle in these two e-books works because the two topics have fairly legitimate associations with sex.

Here's another example of an association that works well: I live in the Boston area, and we (still) have a huge tunnel under construction in a project called the "BigDig." WebEx runs campaigns that offer anyone affected by the BigDig traffic the opportunity to use WebOffice for free and not have to drive into the city. That's a great association, because the traffic situation can be frustrating, and WebEx helps people solve the problem.

YOUR CHALLENGE: How can you push the envelope of what's tried and true in your market? The sex angle certainly isn't for everyone, but are there other subjects you could incorporate in your efforts that others are too scared to talk about?

A LOCAL WORLD WIDE RAVE

Sometimes a World Wide Rave is not worldwide at all but, rather, a localized phenomenon. It's not at all unusual for your buyer persona to be defined by a regional or community issue. For example, hundreds of residents of Janesville, Wisconsin, make use of a local green space called Palmer Park. In particular, dogs (and their human companions) enjoy the beautiful park because a dog can frolic there, off-leash, with other canine friends. Tom Edwards has frequented the park since 1999 with Boo, his German shepherd, and Skip, a fox red Labrador retriever owned by a neighbor. "Lots of people use the eighty-acre wooded park, not only dog owners but also hikers and cross-country skiers," Edwards says. "It's a beautiful place with lots of animals. It's a special place. The other day, Skip kicked up several deer."

In mid-2007, Edwards and other dog walkers were surprised when a sign popped up at the park entrance saying that the city of Janesville was going to put up an aquatic center with a swimming pool on the spot in Palmer Park that Boo, Skip, and so many other dogs and humans enjoy. "We learned that the city had been planning the aquatic center for several years," Edwards says. "But we already have a pool on the other side of town, and nearby Madison has an aquatic center. So we agreed that we would fight the city and its plans. Someone posted a sign with the names and email addresses of city council members so people could complain directly, but the city tore the sign down." When the sign was installed a second time and was removed again, Edwards knew he had to marshal support in other, more innovative ways.

Edwards took the fight online by building a web site ("I knew that they couldn't tear that down," he says). The site,[26] found at the memorable URL "savethedogpark.com," asks visitors: "Does it make sense to turn the pet exercise training area at Palmer Park into a multi-million-dollar aquatic center?" It also features beautiful photos of Boo, Skip, and other dogs romping in the park in all kinds of weather, comments from people who use the space, contact information for city legislators, an email list for people who want updates, and links to local news coverage. There's also an online petition[27] that quickly swelled to hundreds of names.

"The police started harassing me, and I was getting nasty calls from the city council telling me to go away," Edwards says. "One day, the police showed up at the park and said that everyone who was walking dogs off-leash would be ticketed. So I sent a message to my email list and posted information about the incident, which resulted in lots of complaints directly to the city."

The site Edwards created made an immediate and dramatic impact. Soon after he built it, he reached out to WCLO, the local radio station, as well as the *Janesville Gazette* newspaper. "Two days later, I was interviewed on WCLO, and I posted the audio podcast on the updates page of the site," he says. "And the next day we were in the newspaper, which I also linked to from the site. Someone called me and gave me a tip about a dog-friendly television reporter from WKOW-TV in Madison, Wisconsin, and they were down filming within a couple of days. I uploaded the resulting coverage onto YouTube and posted it on the updates page of the site."

During this period of media interest, Edwards pointed people to his site, where they could sign the petition. He very quickly built a list of

[26] www.savethedogpark.com/
[27] www.savethedogpark.com/Sign_The_Petition.html

over 500 people who supported keeping the space green. Edwards then added online resources, such as a *Washington Post* story about the benefits of dog parks. "I learned dog parks are among the most requested amenities in a community, so this information was important for our supporters," he says. "We were generating so much community interest that the city had to take us seriously."

Unless you live in Janesville, Wisconsin (or nearby Madison), you've never heard of Palmer Park and the fight waged over this beloved dog park. However, if you *are* one of the 59,000 Janesville residents, it's highly likely that you're aware of the issue—all because of one man and his localized World Wide Rave. "After about two months of effort, the city caved and we won," says Edwards. He's convinced that without the ability to muster online support from hundreds of people, Boo, Skip, and their pals would likely have been unable to continue enjoying the park they've loved for years.

PEOPLE WANT TO DO BUSINESS WITH PEOPLE

Do you remember the last time you called a toll-free number and were routed through phone-tree hell ("Press 4 for customer support. Press 5 for sales.") and then had to wait on hold? How did that make you feel? Or consider the web sites you've visited recently. How many were dull and uninspiring and didn't answer any of your questions? Did it feel like these organizations cared about you?

Of course not.

People want to do business with people. We're human, and we crave interaction with people who know us. When you build content especially for your buyer personas, you build a relationship with people before you've even met them.

How about the opposite case? Have you recently visited a company web site or blog and said, "Wow! These guys understand me!" Didn't it make you feel different from the way those boring old sites you usually see do?

When online content seems created by some nameless, faceless corporate entity, it doesn't entice us. And we're just not interested in doing business with that company. A corporate-brochure site will never start a World Wide Rave.

We all want to do business with other humans. We want to know there's a breathing person behind the web site or blog that we're reading. And we want to know that those humans on the other side understand and want to help us. A great site or blog or YouTube video, created especially for us, drives us to action. We *want* to do business with people who understand our problems.

There's no secret to building a World Wide Rave. Start by understanding your buyer personas, *not* by hyping your products and services.

NO
COERCION
REQUIRED

UNSCRUPULOUS MARKETING TECHNIQUES

I was trolling the blog search engine Technorati recently, and a banner advertisement caught my eye. They almost never do. I probably click on one banner out of the tens of thousands I am exposed to each month. This particular banner ad sported a black background, and I was attracted first to the Flying V guitar covered by the universal cross-out symbol for *no*. Then I read the headline: "Parents Against Reprehensible Metal Music."

"Cool," I thought. "Tipper Gore wannabes on the rampage. This will be fun."

As the father of a teenage daughter who listens to indie music, obscure metal subgenres, and songs with "explicit" lyrics, I couldn't wait to share this with her so we could both get a chuckle. A couple of checkboxes accompanied the text. "Does your teen show any of the following signs: Interest in music of the occult. Wears excessive amounts of black."

Um, yup. Check. Lots of black clothing in my house (but on Dad as well).

So I clicked the banner.

Imagine my surprise when the banner linked to a site for the Toyota Matrix automobile. At first I thought the ad server was on the fritz and had misdirected me. But then I realized, holy cow, it's a bait-and-switch banner!

I was immediately incensed. The ploy reminded me of those annoying "You are the 1,000,000th visitor! You won! Click here!" ads.

But after a moment, I began to wonder. How much more extensive was this seemingly phony organization? And had anyone else written about it? So I Googled the phrase "Parents Against Reprehensible Metal Music" and found a nifty little spoof site at www.Parents ForPARMM.com which said: "Our censor sensor is always on high alert!" A handful of bloggers had written about the banner.

I decided to write about it on my blog to ask people what they thought:[28] I asked my blog readers: "So here I am writing about it— promoting the site and no doubt sending them a few thousand more clicks. I guess that's what they wanted, right? Well, then, it worked. But what do you think? Is this a reprehensible bait-and-switch? Or just plain fun? What would the transparency police say?"

Opinions were very mixed:

"Reprehensible? Certainly. Hilarious? Absolutely," rockandrollguru said.

"This type of promotion perpetuates the stereotype that companies and marketers are liars," Steve Johnson said.

"Don't like it. I don't believe there's ever a place for tricking prospects. Ever. That being said, I just got done playing some Metallica on my guitar," Jonathan said.

"I did a double-take also. I don't click ads but I wanted to see what this was all about. It was confusing and it took me a while to make sense of it, but it caught my attention and engaged me. Isn't that what marketing is designed to do?" Raza said.

"My children are not that age yet, but you have to congratulate the thinking with this, sneaky as it is," Luke said.

"Bait and switch. I don't like it," Ryan said.

Other bloggers linked to my post (which became sort of a mini-World Wide Rave, by the way) and soon afterward, something interesting happened. The PARMM site[29] no longer worked. As of this writing, if you go to the site, you get the following message: "Error 403—Forbidden. You tried to access a document for which you don't have privileges." *Hmm. . . .*

As I've thought about this campaign and others like it, I've come to realize that viral marketing has a significant dark side, one that's quite a bit more extensive than I had been aware of.

CAREFUL:
DODGY "VIRAL MARKETING" SUCKS

Colleagues and readers frequently send me examples of *viral marketing* (the name comes from the idea that your marketing spreads like a virus online). Many of these examples are nothing more than advertisements that rely on interruption, bait-and-switch gimmicks, inane games, and frivolous contests. It's the old rules of marketing mindlessly transplanted on the Web. These examples bear no resemblance to what I've called a World Wide Rave. Their trickery and coercion is merely an attempt to sell products. Frankly, this stuff gives all marketing a bad name.

I've also encountered a cadre of viral marketing "experts" (typically working in advertising agencies) who will happily take large amounts of money from naïve and unsuspecting companies to create viral marketing "campaigns." Typically, viral campaigns developed by ad agencies involve

[29] www.parentsforparmm.com/

buying access in the same old ways, such as purchasing an email list to spam or launching a microsite that hosts a print- or TV-style ad.

Worse, some dodgy agencies set up fake viral campaigns where people who are employed or in some way compensated by the agency create videos or blog posts purported to be from a customer. And there have been a number of cases reported where staffers at public relations firms employed by movie studios have written gushing (and anonymous) reviews on The Internet Movie Database.[30]

 Going viral via a World Wide Rave is more authentic—and therefore vastly superior as a marketing tool—than going viral via gimmicks. As a way to spread ideas, silly contests and dishonest trickery are yesterday's game.

Because *viral marketing* has taken on sleazy connotations at many organizations, causing marketers and executives to become increasingly skeptical, I use the phrase *World Wide Rave* instead. I want to draw a clear distinction between, on one hand, the amazing ways that millions of Web users share stories and ideas and, on the other hand, all the bogus blather that lazy or dishonest people are resorting to. A *World Wide Rave* centers on valuable content that spreads because—and only because—people want to share it.

[30] www.imdb.com/

AD AGENCIES BEWARE: YOUR VIRAL CAMPAIGN MAY BE AGAINST THE LAW

Misleading viral marketing techniques have become so widespread that the European Union enacted laws to protect the public from the most deceitful activities. Called the Consumer Protection from Unfair Trading Regulations, the regulations also became UK law in May 2008. The Institute of Practitioners in Advertising (IPA), an industry body and professional institute for leading advertising, media, and marketing communications agencies in the UK, is helping its members come to grips with these new laws' implications. The IPA membership includes about 275 of the top agencies in the UK, representing about 80 percent of all British advertising.

"If advertisers and their agencies ignore the ethics of responsible advertising, the damage to the advertising and marketing industry generally will be considerable, undermining all commercial messages, their effectiveness, and the self-regulatory systems," says Marina Palomba, IPA's legal director.

According to the IPA, one particular clause in the Regulations will make the following activities a criminal offense:

- Seeding positive messages about a brand in a blog without making it clear that the message has been created by, or on behalf of, the brand.

- Using "buzz marketing" specialists to communicate with potential consumers in social situations without disclosing that these people are acting as brand ambassadors.

- Posting viral ads on the Internet in a manner that implies the user is an unaffiliated member of the public.

When I asked Palomba about the Parents Against Reprehensible Metal Music campaign, she was concerned.

"This is the sort of teaser advertising that respectable advertisers will need to take more care about in the future," Palomba said. "This Toyota ad is exactly the sort of thing that you cannot do under the new legislation. It is irritating and misleading. This would have been caught by this new legislation, and, here in the UK, people would certainly want to look into this because Toyota is a big company." In fact, Palomba spends much of her time advising UK advertisers about what they can and cannot do under the legislation.

Advice for generating a World Wide Rave

from Marina Palomba, IPA's legal director

"Unless you make it clear up front that the communication is from an advertiser, it is illegal. This has always been illegal in media such as television and print [where it must be labeled as an *advertorial*]. But in blogs and other online [content], it can be confusing. The point here is that advertisers need to be more careful. We've had advertisers do things that they shouldn't, and now they will need to rethink what they are doing."

VIRAL MARKETING
IS RARELY A WORLD WIDE RAVE

A World Wide Rave is when people are talking about your company because they want to, not because they were coerced or tricked. Thus, a World Wide Rave is very different from what people often refer to as *viral marketing*. While there are certainly many ethical advertising agencies out there, be wary of advertising-focused viral efforts.

NO STRINGS REQUIRED

For your ideas to spread and rise to the status of a World Wide Rave, you've got to give up control. Make your Web content totally free for people to access, with *absolutely no virtual strings attached:* no electronic gates, no registration requirements, and no email address checking necessary.

Yes, this advice will come as a shock to many marketers steeped in the tradition of direct-mail advertising—a form of marketing that always requires disclosure of personal information via a toll-free phone call or business reply card (*BRC* in the lingo of direct-mail gurus). Marketers who learned the ins and outs of buying contact lists, the secret workings of BRCs, and the subtle coercion tactics required when creating "offers" naturally want to transfer these esoteric skills (some might even say "black arts") to the Web. As a result, many folks create valuable and interesting information online and then do exactly the wrong thing to distribute it—require viewers to provide personal information first. This is a terrible strategy to spread your ideas. (However, if your *only* goal is to build a mailing list, then the strategy may still be valid. But how many companies are in the business of merely building a list?). When you make people give an email address to get a whitepaper or watch a video, only a tiny fraction will do so; you will lose the vast majority of your potential audience.

YOUR CHALLENGE: You've got to think in terms of spreading ideas, not generating leads. A World Wide Rave gets the word out to thousands or even millions of potential customers. But only if you make your content easy to find and consume.

You may have noticed a fascinating parallel in the music industry. For decades, selling music has been about *exerting control* over music copyright. Before the Web, it was fairly difficult to find illegal copies of music because you needed the physical record or tape. You had to either ask friends to make a copy or go to a dodgy part of town to find a cassette-tape or CD seller on a street corner. When the Internet made possible the easy dissemination of music, the geniuses in the music industry clamped down in control mode—the only way they know how to market and sell. They forced Napster, a centralized music-sharing service that could have been a boon to the industry, to close. This closure forced illegal copying even further underground, where it is virtually impossible to monitor. Today, many players in the industry patrol YouTube and other sites in order to say "no." Instead of looking at the new medium of electronic content as an opportunity, they see it as threat to the old way of selling.

But if you step back and look at the ways musicians make money besides the recordings—concerts, endorsement deals, merchandise (such as $35 t-shirts), and "souvenir" packaging of the music (booklets included in a CD case, for example), not to mention royalties for the use of music in television, movies, and advertising—you start to suspect that clamping down with rigid controls may not be the best strategy. Think about that: They're trying to prevent the spread of their product!

If I were a music executive (or musician), I'd make much of my music available for free online, and I'd encourage people to share it. I would have the confidence that providing music for free would drive sales of my other products. Many unsigned bands are prospering with this strategy through their own MySpace pages or web sites, and some are finding absolutely tremendous success.

A TOP-TEN UNSIGNED BAND ON MYSPACE

For a terrific example of how losing control (in this case, making music available for free) is a great strategy for aspiring musicians, consider Bec Hollcraft,[31] a 19-year-old with an amazing ability to express, through infectious rock melodies and insightful lyrics, the everyday struggles of her generation. Working with Meredith Brooks, a multi-platinum artists, producer, and songwriter, and Jody Nachtigal, personal manager at Arcadia Group Management (and with the support of her parents), Hollcraft went from being a high school freshman in Portland, Oregon to an emerging artist aspiring to a deal from a major label. Her focus on providing tons of free music on MySpace and her own site, plus free editions of her personal *manga* (Japanese-style comics), generated a World Wide Rave.

Hollcraft and Nachtigal figured that if they became big on MySpace, they could use that as a compelling way to interest the record labels. "Bec's MySpace page[32] has been our most active page in promoting, getting feedback, and staying in contact with both fans and potential fans," Nachtigal says. "Over the last few years, MySpace has been among the first places that record labels, agents, and fans go to check out an artist. The layout is consistent, making it easy to hear the latest music and find the latest updates and touring schedule in a very short time. Today, aspiring musicians or bands who are looking for a record deal, or have decided to release material on their own, have to do a lot of the work that used to be left up to the major labels. Luckily, today there are great tools that artists can use to promote themselves. MySpace was the best vehicle for Bec, because both fans and labels were

[31] http://bechollcraft.com/
[32] www.myspace.com/bechollcraft

spending a lot of time there. We decided that our strategy for shopping [for a record label] or 'going it alone' [publishing and selling music themselves, without a label], would be virtually identical, so we began having Bec spend a lot of time and energy working her MySpace pages. Bec was able to contribute a huge part in furthering her own career and getting an idea of who her supporters are."

Nachtigal focused on Hollcraft's MySpace page as the primary vehicle to get her out into the world and also as a way to gauge her buyers' interest (they're mainly teenage girls). "By reaching out to the vast MySpace community, we were able to see which songs worked well, and which didn't," Nachtigal says. "Most of the time, we posted new songs, images, and videos out there and just watched to see how they responded. We never really marketed any of the music; we just wanted to see what the natural reaction was. The amount of time and effort spent working MySpace was undeniable proof, to both the public and labels, that Bec was an artist who was willing to work very hard toward her career. Most people in the music business know that it is very difficult to have success with [acts that don't] care more about their own careers than anyone else could."

The reaction to Hollcraft's music quickly blossomed into a World Wide Rave. Her MySpace monthly page rank by total views reached Number 3 overall and Number 1 for acoustic artists, while her song *Numb* reached Number 28 on MySpace (out of 3.2 million available tracks) and became the Number 2 rock track and Number 1 acoustic track.

The MySpace success was noticed by more than just Hollcraft's fans. "After a few months of working MySpace, we were contacted by virtually every major label, as well as some great indie labels," Nachtigal says.

"This was an effective way to begin promoting Bec to potential buyers, and the labels saw this." They heard from scouts whom the record labels had hired to scour MySpace for talent; they heard directly from A&R (artists and repertoire) executives; and they even heard from several label presidents.

But Nachtigal and Hollcraft did something very unusual. They decided *not* to sign with a label right away and instead use the Web to make the World Wide Rave even bigger.

Inspired by drawings of Bec that were received from some of her fans, she began writing a manga comic series that is offered for free download on her web site.[33] "We were working with an amazing comic artist, who was really able to capture Bec's full personality," says Nachtigal. "We found that comics were a great way for Bec to show the more extreme sides of herself. After all, you can do anything in a comic."

With many U.S. record labels interested in signing Hollcraft, Nachtigal did something else that may seem strange. "Bec needed both the 'bigger than life' promotion strategy that the major label's machinery was once capable of providing [and] a plan that wasn't stuck in 1985," he says. "It was at this point that I began looking toward Japan as the right place for Bec. The Japanese music label industry is still vibrant, and these labels are still capable of selling albums." Nachtigal first signed Bec to a label in Japan, Sony Music Japan International, as a way to build her experience and increase the intensity of her World Wide Rave.

Called "Becca" or "Beccachan" in Japan, Hollcraft speaks directly to her Japanese fans (again, mainly girls and young women) via her Japanese web site[34] and social media sites. The content on her Japanese site is

[33] http://bechollcraft.com/comics/BecComicBlk_1-3.pdf
[34] http://beccachan.com

uploaded directly from Sony Japan, and is mainly written in Japanese. It includes music download links, touring and promotion updates, her latest music videos, and links to Japanese interviews and blogs. "Becca uses a blog, *The Diary of Lady B,*[35] to speak directly to her Japanese fans about her personal life and to give a behind-the-scenes look at her music career," Nachtigal says. She writes all the entries, and they are translated into Japanese, with both the original English and Japanese translation available on the blog.

Sony Japan has focused a great deal of attention on the cell phone market as a major way to sell and promote Hollcraft's music. "Many of the sites most visited by the youth in Japan are cell phone based," Nachtigal says. "The cell phone is extremely sophisticated in Japan, and many of the sales of her music are via cell phone downloads." "Beccachan" has been featured on many different cell phone sites (alas for North American readers, most can't be fully accessed via our inferior cell phone technology).

After coming off a summer 2008 tour of Japan, and making deals for Becca's songs to be used as theme music for several animated Japanese television programs, Nachtigal and Hollcraft are now considering offers for a North American label release. But they've been careful not to define her *too much* through her various social media sites, because a major label's marketing efforts may shape Hollcraft and her image in a different direction with offline marketing and promotion. Nachtigal is certain that the label they eventually sign with will appreciate the World Wide Rave already created in English on social media sites like MySpace (and the buzz in Japan), but he also knows that the label will be eager to craft her offline image according to their own strategies.

[35] http://blog.excite.co.jp/beccachan

Advice for generating a World Wide Rave

from Jody Nachtigal, personal manager at Arcadia Group Management

"Through exploring some of the great new media tools that are available online today, we decided to take the time to consult the experts, the experts being the public—the people who are actually in charge of deciding whether they want to buy what you are selling. In our case, a lot of these new social, networking, blog pages, and other great Web tools are very easy to create, but the really effective results have come from spending a lot of time and energy on them once they are up and running.

It can take a bit of time, but finding out who is really interested in you, and why, is crucial for an artist. Social networks seem to be different [from offline marketing]. If something doesn't work, fix it and try again. There is so much room for experimenting and learning here."

* *

As the Bec Hollcraft World Wide Rave illustrates, offering totally free stuff (in her case, music downloads, manga comics, photos, videos, and more) drives interest. If Hollcraft and her management team had used the old command-and-control methods of the past and limited access to All Things Bec, she'd likely be just another teenager finishing high school. Instead, because of free content and a World Wide Rave that started in the

United States and then spread to Japan, and which will come full-circle back to a major U.S. record label soon, she's an up-and-coming young superstar.

THE GRATEFUL DEAD? OR LED ZEPPELIN?

This idea of offering free access to music to promote artists is not new. Starting in the 1960s, the Grateful Dead encouraged concertgoers to record their live shows, establishing "taper sections" where fans' equipment could be set up for the best sound quality. The band was happy to have Deadheads trade tapes and make copies for friends. The cult of the Grateful Dead concert became a pre-Internet World Wide Rave, driving millions of fans to the band's live shows for over 30 years and generating hundreds of millions of dollars in revenue.

Contrast the Grateful Dead and their open attitude to that of Led Zeppelin and their current label, Warner Music Group. The BBC reports that 20 million people wanted to purchase tickets to the historic Led Zeppelin reunion show held at the O2 Arena on December 10, 2007. Needless to say, the single show left many disappointed fans unable to witness the band's first stage performance in 19 years.

Immediately after the show, grainy, low-fidelity clips appeared on YouTube and were eagerly watched by fans. I was one—hoping to see how the band had changed since I'd seen them as a teenager in June 1977 at New York City's Madison Square Garden. Alas, Warner pulled down the clips within hours, claiming copyright infringement.

These music executives actively tried to stop a World Wide Rave!

In my opinion, they completely underestimate a fan base's power to help sell legal recordings and drive interest in a band. I am absolutely confident that the buzz generated by the concerts sold millions of dollars' worth of Led Zeppelin recordings in the weeks after the concert. The availability of YouTube clips would have enhanced sales. Bands and labels shouldn't worry about low-quality fan tributes. I, for one, am replacing my vinyl recordings with Led Zeppelin CDs, and I'm sure many other people are as well. And all because we've been briefly re-exposed to the power of this band, which we may have ignored for several decades, via fleeting images of a concert we would have traveled halfway around the world to see if tickets had been available.

The music industry needs to rethink its knee-jerk legal impulses to clamp down on fans with draconian measures and to consider instead the power of the Web to sell music. Lighten up. Fans are promoting bands for you—for free. If you want to remain relevant in an always-on, fan-centric, YouTube world, you need to embrace—not restrict—your most important supporters. You need to believe in the power of a World Wide Rave to sell your music.

Of course, the music world serves as just one example. The same ideas apply to all Web content. John Wiley & Sons, the publisher of this book, was thrilled when I made parts of it (and my previous books) available for free on my blog, on other people's blogs, and in magazines. I'm happy to give away free e-books, write a blog, and allow people to record my speeches—all techniques that help my ideas spread. My publisher and I know that free content sells books because people love to get a taste of what they will be buying. The free publicity that's generated by a World Wide Rave can be worth millions of dollars, and if you insist on maintaining control, you're missing a tremendous opportunity to harness that power.

YOUR CHALLENGE: Think about how your information spreads online. If you are clamping down and exerting control, then your ideas aren't spreading as they could be. Consider what valuable content you can offer totally free.

A WORLD WIDE RAVE IS NOT ABOUT SALES LEADS

I'm often confronted with the issue of how to measure an online initiative's results. Executives at companies large and small as well as marketing and PR people push back on the ideas of a World Wide Rave because they want to apply old rules of measurement to the new world of spreading ideas online.

The *old rules of measurement* used two metrics that don't matter when spreading ideas, especially online:

1. We measured "leads"—how many business cards we collected; how many people called the toll-free number; how many people stopped at the tradeshow booth; and how many people filled out a form on our web site, providing their email address and other personal information.

2. We measured "press clips"—the number of times our company and its products were mentioned in mainstream media like magazines, newspapers, radio, and television.

While applying these forms of measurement might be appropriate offline, using them to track your success on the Web just isn't relevant; they don't capture the way ideas travel. Worse, the very act of tracking leads hampers the spread of ideas. People know from experience that if they supply their personal information to an organization, they're likely to get unwanted phone calls from salespeople or to find themselves on email marketing lists. Most won't bother. In fact, I have evidence from several companies that have offered content both with and without a registration requirement that when you eliminate the requirement of supplying personal information in order to receive something, the number of downloads or views goes up by as much as a factor of 50. That's right—if you require an email address or other personal information, perhaps only 2 percent of your audience will bother to download your stuff. Obsessing over sales leads and press clips is likely to be counterproductive and is highly likely to lead to failure of your World Wide Rave.

 For decades, companies have created Web content as lead bait. But the goal should be to get the word out about your organization, not to misuse the Internet for the sake of an outdated technique.

Similarly, measuring success by focusing only on the number of times mainstream media writes or broadcasts about you misses the point. If a blogger is spreading your ideas, that's great. If ten people email a link to your content to their networks or post about you on their Facebook page, that's amazing. You're reaching people, which was the point of seeking media attention in the first place. But most PR people measure only traditional media like magazines, newspapers, radio, and TV, and this practice doesn't capture the value of sharing.

To create a World Wide Rave, forget about sales leads and ignore mainstream media. Instead, focus on spreading your ideas. Make your information totally free, with no registration required.

Here are some questions to ask that can help you measure a World Wide Rave:

1. How many people are exposed to your ideas?
2. How many people are downloading your stuff?
3. How often are bloggers writing about you and your ideas?
4. (And what are those bloggers saying?)
5. Where are you appearing in search results for important phrases?
6. How many people are engaging with you and are making the choice to speak to you about your offerings?

YOUR CHALLENGE: Use Web analytics software to measure how many people are accessing the information on your site and decide whether you're satisfied with the number. If not, how can you publish something that people will want to link to? Finding the answer could dramatically increase the number of people who visit your site, thrilling your bosses in the process.

RETURN ON INVESTMENT IS JUST AN EXCUSE

Once you understand that the metrics of a World Wide Rave are different from what marketers typically measure, you'll need to think differently about *ROI* (return on investment). I often get pushback from executives who insist on exact measurements, in financial terms, of their marketing ROI. It seems that business schools teach their students to obsess over measurement and insist that marketing results be measured in the same way that you'd measure electricity use at company headquarters or revenue from the Canadian market. These executives want to know exactly how much revenue each dollar spent on marketing is producing, and they want to see it in precise campaign-by-campaign spreadsheets.

This trend is causing marketers to become too cautious and boring. Measuring ROI on everything means choosing techniques like direct-mail programs, where you can measure *exactly* how many business reply cards are returned. While that information is useful, it often means that marketers won't invest in creating a World Wide Rave, solely because traditional measurement data are not available.

 For many executives, an obsession with ROI is just a convenient excuse to not try something new and untested. Yet that's exactly what the best ideas for creating a World Wide Rave are—new and untested.

Here's a contradiction. The same executives who insist on ROI measurements from marketing departments happily invest huge sums of money on other things whose returns are also incalculable from an ROI perspective, like the lobby of the building, the fresh coat of paint in the hallway, or even the accounting staff. When CEOs and executives push back with an ROI excuse, I ask, "What's the return on investment of the army of landscapers who are constantly at work on the plantings around your corporate headquarters?" Usually my question is met with embarrassment.

Take a chance. Make the assumption that if millions of people are sharing your ideas (that's a number you can measure), then some percentage of them will buy your products.

BUT WE CAN'T DO THAT!

I also get lots of questions and comments about implementing a World Wide Rave in a corporate environment. People say things like "But we're a _____ company. We can't do things like put a video on YouTube!" (Fill in the blank with "big" or "famous" or "conservative" or "business-to-business" or "nonprofit" or "sports team" or whatever excuse you've got.) The fact is that some of the best World Wide Rave efforts come from unlikely sources.

One of my favorite videos is a series of "mockumentaries" produced by IBM. The multi-episode *The Art of the Sale* is a terrific spoof on corporate training videos. Until the end of the video, you don't even know who produced it. Hundreds of thousands of people have watched the series, humanizing a large company in the process.

"We did an internal video in 2004 for our sales meeting," says Tim Washer, manager of new media web video at IBM Communications. "It was the key things that people needed to know in 2005, but it also included some laughter. It went really well and people liked it, so in summer

2006 I asked the VP of communications if we could make some videos for external use."

Washer and his colleagues at IBM produced the entire video series in-house. "We wanted the videos to make sense for broad sales and corporate audiences," he says. "Many people have seen *The Office*, so they get the concept of a 'mockumentary.' We wrote the scripts and cast the actors—all are IBMers, including the series star, Bob Hoey, who really is the vice president of worldwide sales for System Z, the IBM Mainframe. Lessons one, two, and three were all shot in just a day-and-a-half at our IBM offices."

The first three episodes came out in August 2006. Washer put them onto YouTube[36] and linked to them from the IBM Mainframe blog.

"We originally sent the video to friends in a very informal way," Washer says. "We also included it in one of the IBM newsletters to the sales team, and that helped it to go viral. Then some bloggers picked it up and pushed it along some more."

Washer wasn't surprised when the videos started to take off via word-of-mouse. "Humor always works," he says. "These videos are self-deprecating humor. There are often a lot of barriers to doing this kind of thing within organizations, but to be successful it is critical that this not be done by committee. We're lucky because IBM is big on trusting employees, and they trusted us to do something that would work. The self-deprecation softens the image of IBM with many people—it puts a human face on IBM because we can laugh at ourselves."

Mainstream media also picked up on the videos with some comments on what the use of humor does for IBM's reputation. For example, an article titled "What are they drinking in Armonk?" appeared on the *San Francisco*

[36] www.youtube.com/watch?v=MSqXKp-OOhM

Chronicle blog[37] and said, "You've gotta see this video! . . . IBM is re-positioning the mainframe as a back-to-the-future alternative. The tone of Hoey's spoof training video is in keeping with the kinder, humbler image IBM now seeks to project."

Some of the ways that these *The Art of the Sale* videos have spread virally have been surprising to Washer. "Our first series was selected as one of Comedy Central's 'Staff Favorites,'" he says. "We even got requests from other large companies, such as Price Waterhouse, to show our videos at their sales conferences!"

Washer had the videos translated into several different languages, including Japanese. "This approach works in many cultures because many things within the video itself are visual."

The fourth, fifth, and sixth installments of *The Art of the Sale* were launched in November 2007 on the IBM Mainframe blog.[38]

With these videos' success in reaching hundreds of thousands of people and improving IBM's corporate image, Washer is very surprised that more companies haven't followed his example. "I thought that so many people would be using humor, but it just hasn't happened yet," he says.

---

[37] www.sfgate.com/cgi-bin/blogs/sfgate/detail?blogid=19&entry_id=8367
[38] mainframe.typepad.com/blog/2007/11/mainframe-on-yo.html

Advice for generating a World Wide Rave

from Tim Washer, manager of new media web video, IBM Communications

"When producing a viral video, enlist the best artists and storytellers on the team, and give them license to create a compelling, engaging spot that may have nothing to do with the brand or message points. Spend your thirty-to-ninety seconds entertaining the audience instead of forcing message points. Be willing to experiment with a video that might not be consistent with your brand image. Most likely, you'll have a better chance to reach a new, different audience on YouTube if the video is 'off-brand.'"

....

SOLD OUT, SO WHAT!

For another interesting use of video, check out those produced by Max Deale, author of the book *Sold Out, So What! The Secrets that High-Priced Ticket Brokers and Scalpers DON'T want you to Know!*[39] The book is for fans of concerts and sporting events and teaches the art of scoring tickets to sold-out events, and always sitting in the best seats in the house. Deale, known to his friends as the "Ticket Jedi," spent 20 years perfecting his technique of acquiring "sold-out" tickets at or below face value. (One of his themes is that there is no such thing as "sold-out.") He calls his video series[40] "ridiculously idiotic spoof commercials," and says: "I'll

[39] www.soldoutsowhat.net/
[40] www.youtube.com/soldoutsowhat

keep pumping them out until I get it right." My personal favorite is called "The Scalper's Got My Baby." It's amazing what you can produce with a little time and a healthy dose of creativity. As a result of his site and the videos, Deale was recently interviewed for an article in *Rolling Stone*, and *Sold Out, So What!* is selling briskly.

YOUR CHALLENGE: Every company has something fascinating, or unique, or funny that can be turned into a video that people will want to share. You do, too. What's that one thing that everyone who knows you comments about? Build your video efforts around that.

ONLINE VIDEO AND THE WORLD WIDE RAVE

Before YouTube made video commonplace on the Web, you'd only see small forays into corporate video, and usually these efforts were mundane and predictable—stuff like broadcasts of the CEO's speech at the annual meeting. Well, okay, some people might have watched, but unless the CEO made a dramatic gaffe (picking his nose while talking, perhaps), a video like that was highly unlikely to spread like wildfire.

Now, creating and publishing a simple video is really easy; all that's required is a basic digital video camera and a YouTube account. There are all sorts of available enhancements and editing techniques to make video look more professional, but some organizations prefer to go with the grainy and jerky "homemade" look. Other companies (like IBM) create a regular series of videos that might be delivered through a video blog (vlog), an online video channel at a company site, or a *vodcast* (a video series syndicated with iTunes or RSS feeds).

Nine tips for using YouTube to generate a World Wide Rave

Ready to try out your production skills on YouTube? Here are some things to keep in mind:

1. Creating a video is easy, and posting on YouTube is free.

Shoot the video using a digital video camera and copy it to your computer. You can then either upload the video to YouTube as is or edit it with software such as iMovie or Windows Movie Maker to add titles and special effects. You might shoot from different angles with one or more cameras and then piece together the footage to create a unified final product. But remember, less is usually more when it comes to special effects. When you're ready to upload the video, you just need to create a free YouTube account and follow the directions to add the video.

2. Homemade is just fine.

You don't need to hire a professional. A homemade-quality video can work well and is sometimes preferable. We're bombarded with over-produced TV commercials all the time—so often that we usually just turn off our minds when they come on. An authentic and interesting video (rather than a slick and polished one) in which your personality shines through can make people notice. But plan ahead and shoot several takes to get it right.

3. Your video should be no longer than three minutes (preferably shorter).

Think very short. When people watch video, they have extremely short attention spans. There are millions of videos on YouTube, and it's very easy to click away from yours. Although YouTube will accept videos up to 10 minutes (smaller than 100 MB), try to make yours between

30 seconds and 2 minutes. If you have more to say, consider creating a series of videos rather than making one that's too long.

4. Make your description clear and specific.

A critical component of your video will be its title—the name the world will associate with your work—so think carefully about it. Make it descriptive and unique. To best promote your video, create an accurate and interesting text blurb. Use descriptive keywords and language that people will use when they search for videos like yours.

5. Don't attempt "stealth" fake customer insertions.

Some companies attempt sneaky stealth insertions of corporate-sponsored videos that are made to appear consumer-generated. A typical case might feature happy 20-somethings at a party having fun while using products of a certain brand. The YouTube community is remarkably skilled at ratting out inauthentic video, so this approach is likely to backfire and cause harm to a brand. Remember, if your video is worth watching, viewers won't care that it was submitted by a company.

6. Consider inviting your customer communities to submit video.

One of the most effective ways to use video to drive a World Wide Rave is for companies to develop a contest in which users submit their own video, which then is made available for others to see. The best would-be directors are given prizes, and their videos are usually showcased on the company site. In some cases, the winning videos are also played on TV as "real" commercials. For example, more than 100 people submitted videos for a Mentos contest seeking the best customer-created videos of geysers made by combining the popular mints with Diet Coke.[41]

[41] www.youtube.com/group/mentosgeysercontest

7. Try a series of similar videos to build interest.

Sometimes a series of videos, such as those from Blendtec, a small company that makes household blenders, works well. Blendtec created a huge World Wide Rave (one that you've likely heard of) with their series of YouTube videos called "Will It Blend?" If you haven't seen examples of these videos yet, check them out. The following videos have each been viewed more than a million times:

- Will It Blend? iPhone[42]
- Will It Blend? Golf Balls[43]
- Will It Blend? Marbles[44]

Another example of a successful video series comes from Wine Library,[45] an online wine merchant. On Wine Library TV, Gary Vaynerchuk breaks down the barriers, stereotypes, and misperceptions about wine in a daily video series. Through his unconventional, often irreverent commentary on wine (he routinely interrupts some episodes with rants about his beloved New York Jets), Vaynerchuk has attracted a cult-like following of more than 80,000 viewers per day.

8. Tell everyone about your video!

When you upload your first few videos, you are likely to hear a deafening silence. You'll be waiting for comments, but none will come. You'll check your video statistics and be disappointed by the tiny number of viewers. Don't get discouraged—that's normal! It takes time to build an audience. When you're just getting started, make sure people know it's there and can find it. Create links to your video from your homepage, product pages, or online media room. Mention your video in your email or offline newsletters, and create links to your video as part of your email signature and those of other people in your organization.

[42] www.youtube.com/watch?v=qg1ckCkm8Yl
[43] www.youtube.com/watch?v=qg1ckCkm8Yl
[44] www.youtube.com/watch?v=3OmpnfL5PCw
[45] http://winelibrary.com/

9. Make sure bloggers know about the video.

Sending bloggers a link to the video or commenting on other people's blogs (and including a link to your video) is a good way to build an audience. If you comment on blogs in the same market category as yours, you might be surprised at how quickly you will get viewers to your video. However, when commenting on someone else's blog real estate, make sure you're on topic and genuinely contributing to the conversation in addition to linking to your video. Don't just spam bloggers with your link without adding value.

Above all, have fun! Don't be afraid to go out there and experiment.

Video content on the Web is still very new for marketers and communicators. But the potential to deliver information to buyers in new and surprising ways is greater when you use a new medium. And while your competition is still trying to figure out "that blogging thing," you can tap into the world of video and leave the competition behind.

LET'S BE HONEST

I want to turn our attention now to the issue of how organizations choose to embrace (or more likely resist) sharing ideas online. The idea of customers and employees spreading "marketing messages" for an organization via blogs, forums, chat rooms, and other social media sites such as YouTube scares many marketers, corporate communications people, and company executives to death! For decades, companies have figured out ways to control their messaging, typically by clamming up and not saying much—except, that is, for a handful of authorized and highly trained spokespeople like the public relations director and the CEO. Companies have used one-way communications, mostly advertising and press releases, to issue formal announcements and have generally forbidden rank-and-file employees from saying anything at all.

Before we go any further, let's define the term *social media*, which most people have heard of but which not everybody understands. The term describes the way people share ideas, content, thoughts, and relationships online. Social media differ from so-called "mainstream media" in that anyone can create, comment, and add to social media content. Social media can take the form of text, audio, video, images, and communities, and the technologies of social media include blogging software, podcast tools, wiki software, message boards, virtual communities, and networking tools.

As the tools of social media have enabled anybody (company insiders as well as customers and critics) to say anything about a company, many organizations have persisted in the old command-and-control methods of the past, clamping down with rules and regulations that prohibit employees from communicating online. Just as bad, many organizations ignore what appears about their company on blogs, forums, and social media sites.

Okay, let's be honest. Marketers and executives aren't really scared of social media and the idea of a World Wide Rave. They are scared of the unknown. People are comfortable doing the same old rubbish year in and year out. They spend tons of money at tradeshows. They spam their customers with inane email "campaigns" that typically include "offers" such as free shipping or some sort of discount pricing. They invest in television commercials and Yellow Page ads. They pay PR agencies the big bucks to get a mention on page 60 of a local newspaper, a laundry-list inclusion in an analyst's report, or a quote in the tenth paragraph of a story in a trade magazine that almost nobody reads. Then they say, "*Woo hoo!*," celebrating that they scored press "hits."

Think about the last few products you purchased. Did you answer a direct-mail ad? Go to a tradeshow to learn more? Turn to the Yellow Pages? As I mentioned earlier, if you're like most people, you didn't do any of those things—you went online. So why are we marketing in the same old ways?

If we're really honest, we must realize that buying access with expensive advertising and communicating exclusively through the media and analysts is not an effective online strategy.

What works online is creating content ourselves—information that people want to share. And we should be encouraging our employees, customers, and other interested stakeholders to tell our stories and spread our ideas. We should be celebrating blogs, forums, and the tools of social media, not clamping down on them.

If we're totally honest, we must know that we no longer control the sales process. We need to realize that today's consumer skepticism means that to depend on million-dollar direct-mail campaigns targeting the top sales prospects, big-budget advertisements that cast too wide a net, or message-driven PR campaigns directed at media insiders who reach fewer readers and viewers than they once did, is to risk failure and irrelevancy.

People research answers to their problems by turning first to Google and other search engines. A great way to reach people there is to trigger a World Wide Rave, spreading your ideas so that people find you.

BLOCK SOCIAL MEDIA SITES
AT YOUR OWN PERIL

I've had an opportunity to casually explore the attitudes of hundreds of large and small companies whose employees attend my full-day New Rules of Marketing seminar and my keynote speeches. Based on my very unscientific show-of-hands surveys, I'd estimate that more than 25 percent of companies block employee access to YouTube, Facebook, and other social networking sites.

More than 25 percent block access!

That is a huge number of companies putting themselves at a disadvantage. I can't tell you the names of these nanny-state dinosaurs, but you'd be amazed at some of the big players that are too scared to let their employees into the world of social media. If I managed a hedge fund, I'd sell short a basket of stock from companies that block social media and buy companies that, like IBM, encourage employee use of these new tools.

Here are some of the reasons companies give for blocking access to sites like YouTube and Facebook:

- It is a drain on productivity because people using these sites or participating on forums, chat rooms, and blogs are not doing "real work."

- It is a security issue within the company computer systems, because people are logging onto sites outside the corporate firewall.

- Employees may harm the company brand should they reveal too much information. (*Gasp!* These sites allow open access, so anyone can see anything!)

- It is a bandwidth issue; companies would need to purchase a more robust Internet service infrastructure.

DO YOU TRUST YOUR EMPLOYEES?

I think the real issue here is about trust, and the reasons company representatives give, like all that baloney about ROI, are just excuses. Ultimately, I think human resources and legal departments are naïve and scared about what their corporate charges might do out in the wide world of the Web. Since HR and legal people don't usually understand social media themselves (and don't use them for business in their jobs), they respond by just slapping on controls.

YOUR CHALLENGE: You can't generate a World Wide Rave if your employees are forbidden from accessing the sites to trigger one. If you trust your employees, they might surprise you with the ways they promote your business on social media sites. But if you don't trust them, you end up with only the corporate dregs—workers who don't mind submitting to an organization that won't let them communicate the way people do today.

WE'RE TALKING ABOUT PEOPLE, NOT TECHNOLOGY

This debate about social media in the enterprise is just so damn silly. It seems crazy to me to try to regulate technology in the workplace when the real harm (or benefit!) comes from the people using that technology. I've witnessed the same phenomena twice in the past two decades: when personal computers entered the workplace in the 1980s, and during the Web and email debates of the 1990s. If you were in the workforce at the time, you might recall when executives believed email would expose a corporation's secrets, and therefore only "important employees" (often defined as director-level and above) were given computers and email addresses. Years later (beginning in 1994), companies fretted about employees freely using the public Internet and being exposed to "unverified information" that was not written by "real journalists."

The solution has always been the same: Don't provide employees with computers. Refuse to provide a company email address. Ban the Internet within the corporate firewalls. Block YouTube, Facebook, blogs, and forums from view. Yet how many companies today refuse to provide a computer to employees at work if it can help them do their job? How many don't provide company email? How many ban Internet access completely? Virtually none. So why are companies falling into the same old foolish patterns?

It's just silly to forbid employees access to computers, email, and the Web. Yet the exact same debate—in the same language from a decade ago—is now raging about access to social media. Don't be silly yourself and fall into a debate about technology. Instead focus on people.

My recommendations to organizations are simple: Have guidelines about what you can and cannot do at work. Hold employees to a measurable standard for performance on the job. But don't try to ban a specific set of social media technologies. Your guidelines should include advice about how to communicate in any medium, including face-to-face conversation, presentations at events, email, social media, online forums and chat rooms, and other forms of communication. Rather than putting restrictions on social media (the technology), it's better to focus on guiding the way people behave. The corporate guidelines could inform employees that they can't reveal company secrets, they can't use inside information to trade stock or influence prices, and they must be transparent and provide their real name and affiliation when communicating.

As long as your employees get their work done in a satisfactory manner, there should be no need to regulate their minute-to-minute behavior. You don't regulate how often people can use the restroom, when they can chat with a colleague in the hallway about their kids, or whether they use a mobile phone for company calls while taking a cigarette break, so why regulate when they can look at an online video? If you have individual cases of people not getting their jobs done in a satisfactory manner, deal with that problem as the "people issue" it really is. If it persists after several warnings, fire the employee, but make sure your expectations were clear from the start.

IBM'S SOCIAL COMPUTING GUIDELINES

Contrast the paranoid nanny-state organizations, which clamp down on their employees, with IBM, a company on the forefront of embracing employee use of social media. IBM has developed a set of social computing guidelines[46] for employee use of blogs, wikis, social networks, virtual worlds, and social media. I think they are just fantastic. Here's a taste:

"Whether or not an IBMer chooses to create or participate in a blog, wiki, online social network or any other form of online publishing or discussion is his or her own decision. However, emerging online collaboration platforms are fundamentally changing the way IBMers work and engage with each other, clients and partners. IBM is increasingly exploring how online discourse through social computing can empower IBMers as global professionals, innovators and citizens. These individual interactions represent a new model: not mass communications, but masses of communicators. Therefore, it is very much in IBM's interest—and, we believe, in each IBMer's own—to be aware of and participate in this sphere of information, interaction and idea exchange."

This is the way of the future. My advice for bosses is to follow IBM's pioneering example.

YOUR CHALLENGE: Get a group together and draft a set of social media guidelines for your company. Get them approved by the legal and communications departments, and then let all employees know about the guidelines to encourage social media participation.

---

[46] www.ibm.com/blogs/zz/en/guidelines.html

NEW YORK ISLANDERS WIN BIG

Another organization that's boldly embracing social media is the New York Islanders professional ice hockey team. The team created what they call the "blog box," providing bloggers with press credentials for select games. The Islanders Blog Box rules are simple:[47] "The NYI Blog Box will be your open forum. From start to finish, you'll be in control. All we ask is for the chosen bloggers to act respectfully in the restricted media areas and keep all critiques in good taste."

The blog box program started at the beginning of the 2007–2008 season and was among the first of its kind for a major professional sports team. About a dozen bloggers were chosen for the credentials the first season, and the team links to their blogs from its site.[48] The popular program will continue in the 2008–2009 season.

"The bloggers are in a press box that has a better view than the traditional press box; they get locker room access to all of our post-game interviews and to our head coach's press conference," says Josh Bernstein, vice president of communications for the New York Islanders. "We arranged for two members of the Blog Box to get press row access at the NHL Draft in Ottawa in June 2008 and gave them one-on-one interviews with our team executives, scouts, and even our draft picks during and after the draft. They break stories on their blogs, get exclusive phone interview time with players, and every other level of access that the 'mainstream' media is accustomed to getting. It's been a ton of fun and a great success."

---

[47]http://islanders.nhl.com/team/app?articleid=318161&page=NewsPage&service=page
[48]http://islanders.nhl.com/blogbox/blog_box.htm

Contrast what the Islanders have done with the vast majority of organizations' strategies. I've found that most communicators are scared to death of bloggers. Executives frequently ask me: "What if they say something negative?" PR people say: "These aren't real journalists. Why should we care about a bunch of geeks in their pajamas?"

Guess what? Bloggers like Frank Trovato[49] (who is a member of Blog Box) were already blogging about the Islanders! Bloggers are likely already talking about *your* organization, too. Why not cultivate a relationship with them?

It's working for the Islanders. Trovato writes: "My goals for this blog are to voice not only my opinions, but the opinions of so many Islander fans that never get the chance to get their opinions heard because of the lack of forums available to us in the media. The Islanders organization continue[s] to provide the fans the opportunity to speak out and be vocal and, no matter what our opinions are, seems to really listen and care what we think."

YOUR CHALLENGE: Think about what your organization can do to work with bloggers (as well as podcasters and video bloggers). Be the first organization in your industry to embrace them by including them in your press conferences, scheduling interviews for them with your executives, or even making them part of your product tests.

DO YOU WORK FOR A COMPANY THAT BLOCKS ACCESS?

If you work for a company that blocks access, I suggest you become an agent of change. Give your bosses a copy of this book. Share the IBM Social Computing Guidelines with your executives. Point them to what the New York Islanders have done. Encourage them not to focus on the (mostly exaggerated) negative sides of social media.

If they still refuse to open up, I suggest you quit your job and work for a company that embraces the new world. You'll need to find a new job anyway, because your company won't be around in a few years; smarter competitors will take away your business by reaching buyers on the Web.

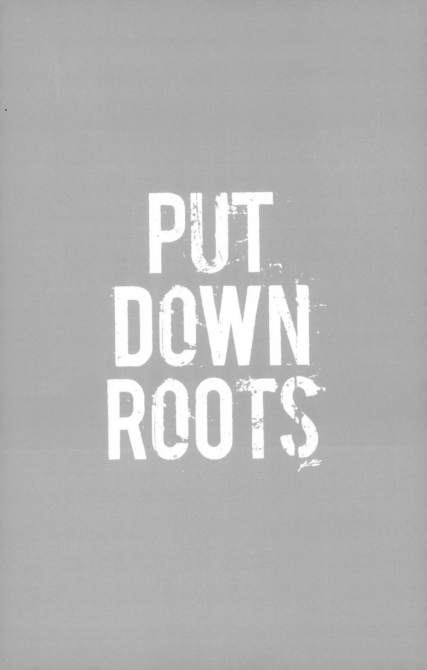
PUT
DOWN
ROOTS

WHEN FRIENDS TRIGGER
A WORLD WIDE RAVE

Participation is required for people to want to tell your stories for you. Think about your own life. You're more likely to tell a story about someone you know than a stranger, right? It the same thing online. If you want your ideas to spread, you need to be involved in the online communities of people who actively share.

One of the best ways to create a World Wide Rave is to use your social network. The people who already know you, your virtual community, are already your supporters; when they see something funny, interesting, or remarkable, they want to share it. There's no easier way to reach people than to use their enthusiasm to help your cause.

In the past several years, Facebook has taken off as an online tool for anyone looking to connect to communities and customers directly. The explosion in popularity was due to the September 2006 opening of Facebook to non-students. Before that date, you needed an e-mail address ending in ".edu" to qualify for an account. According to comScore Media Metrix,[50] in the months prior to allowing open registration, Facebook.com traffic hovered at approximately 14 million unique visitors per month. Visitors nearly doubled in the next nine months, totaling 26.6 million by May 2007. The numbers are significantly higher today.

The site connects members via a "friend request" process. Until you approve someone as your Facebook friend, your extended profile remains private. Many members use Facebook as a way to maintain casual contact with people they meet in person and online. In my own case, I use

---

[50] www.comscore.com/

my circle of friends as a sounding board for new ideas, and I let them know first about the things I'm up to. For example, when I publish a new e-book or hardcover, I post a message on my Facebook page. Similarly, back when I set up my profile, I included a short video to give my Facebook friends an idea of what one of my speeches is like. They see my Facebook updates via their Facebook "feed," which is basically an ongoing summary of information from their circle of friends.

ANYONE CAN TRIGGER A WORLD WIDE RAVE

On November 28, 2007, Steve Jackson[51] started a Facebook group called Six Degrees of Separation.[52] Jackson is the author of the Paul Aston thrillers, *The Mentor* and *The Judas,* and he started the group as research for his newest novel, *The Watcher.* One of the themes he explores in his new book is the way people are connected on the Web, so he planned to use the group as a way of testing how quickly people join up and whether it's possible to connect to every single person on the site. "Facebook is a kind of Internet-in-miniature, which makes it the ideal place to examine this idea," Jackson writes.[53]

His process was really simple. Jackson kicked things off by inviting some of his friends to join. As these and all other potential members visited the group's Facebook page for the first time, potential new members saw the following simple instructions:

[51] www.steve-jackson.net/
[52] www.facebook.com/group.php?gid=8900080125
[53] www.steve-jackson.net/six_degrees/index.html

To take part all you have to do is:
1. Join this group.
2. Click on "Invite People to Join" from the menu on the right.
3. Select all your friends (for the experiment to work, you need to do this).
4. Click on "Send invitation."

By the end of the first day, fewer than 20 of Jackson's friends had joined, but the trigger to spread his World Wide Rave was in place. Things started slowly in terms of absolute numbers—with 200 members by day four and 400 by day five—but the *percentage* growth each day was huge. After a week, the number of members in the group reached 30,000. The next day, 141,000 new members joined. "The next 16 days were a complete rollercoaster ride," Jackson writes. "Sixteen six-figure days in a row! This was completely unprecedented! At times we were adding members at a rate of three every single second. For six days we were averaging 220,000 new members a day." On day 13, the group hit the one-million-member mark and was growing at a rate of almost a quarter of a million per day. Jackson finally noticed the inevitable growth-rate slowdown on day 18. As of this writing, about six months after the start of the experiment, the group boasts 4,736,217 members—including me, and probably some of you as well. Remarkably, many members are active. For instance, they've left some 190,000 messages on the group "wall" for others to see. Jackson's experiment became a truly *World Wide Rave*, with many members creating invitations in their native languages and sharing them with others.

"It was around this time I realised Six Degrees was more than just re-search for my new book," Jackson writes. "This was a truly interna-tional Internet phenomenon! Each day I was getting a load of emails from every corner of the globe. Most people just wanted to tell me how much they enjoyed the group; others had suggestions on how we could improve things. The idea behind Six Degrees of Separation fascinates me—and judging by how many people joined the group, this is a fascination shared by millions of you across the globe. As progress marches on, the world gets smaller. That's inevitable. Whether we're separated by six degrees or ten degrees or one degree isn't important. What is important is the idea that we are connected."

Wow. An author decides to create a Facebook group as an experiment. It probably takes him less than an hour to create. And by the time you read this, well over five million people will likely be members—a World Wide Rave to be sure. If Jackson can do it, so can you.

THOUSANDS OF FANS; ONE RANDOM YOUTH SOCCER TEAM

Still not convinced that anyone can trigger a World Wide Rave? Consider what Swedish entrepreneur Emil Nylander cooked up. Nylander's company, Virality Communication,[54] develops Web-based videos and communications strategies to help people share their ideas. In March 2008, he was involved in an experiment to try to organize 400 people to support a junior soccer team (American readers take note: That's *football* in Sweden). They chose Facebook as the tool for rallying interest and spreading the word. "The idea was to gather a bunch of people and go see a randomly chosen team of ten-year-olds play a football match and become fans of the team," Nylander says. "The group became really popular, and within days more than 3,000 people had joined." The group selected a team to support, the game they would attend, and also what colors they'd wear.

On the big day, the fans were to meet at the central train station so they could all march to the game together. The organizers were surprised when a crowd estimated at nearly 1,000 people turned up, most wearing the chosen color, red, and many carrying various noisemakers to add to the fun. While Nylander and the other group members were surprised by the turnout, the young players on the chosen team, Hässelby, and their opponents, Huddinge, were flat-out amazed at the size of the crowd—for a game usually attended by just parents. Sweden's second largest TV station had also heard about the experiment and sent a crew to do a story that aired that day.[55]

"As an owner of a production company that makes films for the Web, I saw the opportunity to make a fun film about this," Nylander says. "We recorded the whole thing, edited it quickly, and put it on YouTube."[56]

Nylander expected the video to serve as a simple tribute to the young players and the fans who showed up. "Days passed and we pretty much forgot about the whole thing," he says. "Then something happened. People started putting the YouTube video on their blogs, linking to it from other sites, and sending it to their friends via email."

As of this writing, the video has been seen over 50,000 times, and dozens of bloggers have written about it. We're talking about a video of a random football match between ten-year-olds! If something this seemingly unremarkable and mundane can become a World Wide Rave, certainly you've got something that can, too.

Advice for generating a World Wide Rave

from Emil Nylander, president of Virality Communication

"People and companies are finding it more and more difficult to get their voice heard. The Web is the strongest tool available to reach out and tell people about your ideas, create a buzz, and—most importantly—create a spark to involvement. This film we made about the football team really turned out to be a perfect test case, showing what is actually possible to achieve with very few resources and a couple of creative minds.

Companies that have the ability and the will to use the Web in the right way have a lot to gain. It's a fine balance though, because putting a logo on something nowadays immediately causes suspicion. The key for success is honesty, transparency, and not to be an apparent sellout. There are no rules, however, so a gut feeling is vital: How would people react to this? What is our message? Why should people be interested?"

● ●

FACEBOOK APPLICATIONS: WHERE'S YOUR WIDGET?

Clearly, creating a Facebook group can be a great way to trigger a World Wide Rave. Groups like Steve Jackson's Six Degrees of Separation or the group Emil Nylander started to support a Swedish junior soccer team have potential to draw in thousands or even millions of members.

But Facebook offers even more.

One of the best approaches for generating a World Wide Rave on Facebook is to create a Facebook application, which is a great way to build your brand. Facebook applications provide all users the choice to add features that are not part of the standard interface. Recognizing that users want to add additional features, the smart people at Facebook created Facebook Platform,[57] an initiative that developers from around the world use to build new applications for the site. As an open platform, Facebook allows anybody to create applications to help friends share information in different ways. There are currently some 10,000 applications available on Facebook, and the more popular ones are used regularly by hundreds of thousands of people or more. One of my favorites has more than 5 million users! (Not bad for a trigger that costs nothing to launch and is easy to create.)

YOUR CHALLENGE: Facebook applications are all about providing an interesting way for friends to connect and share valuable information. Your business probably lends itself to an entertaining or useful application, too.

HOW MANY CITIES HAVE YOU VISITED?

The best applications for marketers to consider are the ones that help promote the sorts of products and services their companies sell. The "Cities I've Visited" application[58] from TripAdvisor,[59] the world's largest online community for travelers, is one such application. It displays a map on users' Facebook pages where they can stick virtual thumbtacks in the cities they've visited. Sharing stories is half the fun of travel, and Cities I've Visited lets travelers quickly create an interactive map to facilitate sharing and comparing those stories with friends. Cities I've Visited covers more than 20,000 destinations. Since I'm on the road a lot, I also appreciate it as a great way for me to keep track of my own world travel. TripAdvisor's business is providing unbiased hotel reviews, destination photos, and travel advice, so the Cities I've Visited Facebook application is a perfect marketing tool for the company.

Remarkably, *more than five million people have added Cities I've Visited to their Facebook profiles*—a certified World Wide Rave. Since typical Facebook users have hundreds of friends, the exposure for TripAdvisor is enormous. And it's free.

"The Web is going to portable applications and distributed applications, so we thought it would be worthy of the investment to put something out there onto Facebook," says Erik Rannala, vice president for product at TripAdvisor. "We already had a place on TripAdvisor where members could plot their travels, and it was popular on the site. So we thought, why not use this as the basis of something to do on Facebook. So we reworked it as a distributed platform on Facebook and launched in June 2007."

---

[58] www.facebook.com/apps/application.php?id=2219089314
[59] www.tripadvisor.com/

Rannala says it was very easy to build the application and make it live on Facebook. "It was not a huge deal to do because we had a lot of the back-end map functionality already built," he says. "So it really only took a few days to do the initial application." Hang on. I want to make sure you got that. This application took a few days to create, and more than five million people have it on their Facebook page, displaying the application to all of their perhaps hundreds or thousands of friends. Isn't that amazing?

"A lot of people saw Cities I've Visited on someone else's profile or saw it in the application directory and then put it on their profile," Rannala says. "It went viral because people saw it on their friends' Facebook page."

Of course, the considerable benefit for TripAdvisor is that over five million people have, at least implicitly, endorsed the company by making the tool a part of their online identity. "On some level, there is a huge brand impact," Rannala says. "So it is a very strong endorsement. Our branding is very subtle, but it is apparent to most people that it [the application] is from TripAdvisor. There are links back to TripAdvisor so people can get to our site. And this has become one of the top sources of new members to the main TripAdvisor site, where we have more than ten million consumer reviews and opinions. These are people who can read and interact with our millions of travel guides, reviews, forum posts—all generated by consumers."

Advice for generating a World Wide Rave

from Erik Rannala, vice president of product for TripAdvisor

"You have to make it fun and immediately relate to people. In our case, you can see your friends' top destinations—where they have been and where they are going. This is very interesting stuff for social networks. You also need to provide things for people to come back. For example, we alert you when your friends have been or are going to one of your favorite places. One of the primary ways that this is different from standard marketing is that it is free. Getting onto the Facebook platform is free. It takes some time (and maybe money) to make, but you can reach millions of people for free!"

. . . .

ARE YOU ON TWITTER YET?

Are you on Twitter[60] yet? This question comes up again and again and is sometimes used as code for "Are you hip to social media?" Twitter is the most popular "microblogging" service and is used for friends, family, and coworkers to communicate through the exchange of quick, frequent updates about what you're up to. If you're already on Twitter, feel free to skip this section. However, if you've never experimented with this tool, you might be puzzled as to what the fuss is all about. Think of it as an instant message (IM) that is broadcast to everyone in your network. I know many people quickly become addicted to sending out "tweets" (microblog posts with a maximum of 140 characters).

People use Twitter to keep their "followers" (people who subscribe to their Twitter feed) updated on their life. For instance, you might tweet about whom you're having a beer with after work, or you might ask your network a question. I update my Twitter feed[61] a few times a day, tweeting about my travels around the world, whom I'm meeting, what I think is cool, and what's going on at the conferences and events that I speak at. Over five thousand people follow my activities this way. Users can choose to follow the Twitter updates of anyone they want to hear from: family members, colleagues, or perhaps the author of the last book they read (hint, hint).

Twitter is a great way to trigger a World Wide Rave and to push existing buzz along. During the 2008 presidential campaign, Barack Obama[62] updated nearly 100,000 followers about his daily travels. In fact, Obama's followers who kept up with his campaign via Twitter were among the first to learn of his choice for vice president.[63] The Obama campaign alerted supporters via social media first, before they issued a press release to the media. Of course, savvy reporters expected this and subscribed to his Twitter feed.

Companies use Twitter to update customers in real-time. For example, Dell Outlet[64] uses Twitter to promote special deals on refurbished Dell computer equipment and electronics. BosTix.org, a program of Arts

[61] http://twitter.com/dmscott
[62] http://twitter.com/barackobama
[63] http://twitter.com/BarackObama/statuses/883563719
[64] http://twitter.com/DellOutlet

Boston[65] that provides discount tickets for theater, music, and dance for over 100 greater Boston arts organizations, alerts followers on Twitter about updates on reviews, and special ticket offerings.[66] They also offer the service via other social media sharing sites including Pownce[67] and Utterz.[68] Fans of the arts can be sure that they have the latest information about ticket availability via the social media services they prefer. A bit later in the book, you'll meet a residential real estate agent who created a World Wide Rave and found a hot new job via Twitter.

SOCIAL NETWORKING AND A WORLD WIDE RAVE

Social networking sites like Facebook, Twitter, and the many other similar sites require participation. While I discuss Facebook and Twitter in these pages, there are hundreds of other social networking sites to explore. The best ones for your organization are the sites that your buyer personas are active in today.

Participation is not about promoting your products and services like an advertiser does. Rather, as a full participant in a virtual community, you create a profile for yourself, participate in (and establish) groups, and maybe even develop an application. I really can't stress enough that without taking steps to 'put down roots' in a virtual community, you'll never be taken seriously. In fact, you may be ridiculed if you swoop in without having already developed a presence.

[65] www.artsboston.org/
[66] http://twitter.com//artsboston
[67] http://pownce.com/
[68] www.utterz.com/

Here are some ideas to generate a World Wide Rave using social networking:

- **Have fun.** Members want to interact with people they like.
- **Join.** Encourage everyone in your organization to create personal profiles on Facebook, Twitter, and/or MySpace (or whatever social networking sites make sense in your country or market).
- **Participate.** Be an online thought leader by creating and hosting a group. Provide valuable and interesting information that people want to check out. Show your expertise in a market and people will flock to you.
- **Target.** Create groups or applications that reach an audience that is important to your organization. It's usually better to target a niche market than to try to reach the entire Facebook community.
- **Be available.** Encourage people to contact you, and create links so people can get to your other online content (like your web site and your blog).
- **Experiment.** These are great online playgrounds for trying new things.

YOUR CHALLENGE: If you aren't on Facebook and Twitter already, create profiles for yourself. Do it today—it takes less than an hour to get going. Then interview your buyer personas to learn what other social networking sites are popular with them and build profiles on those sites, too.

WORLD WIDE RANT:
WHEN BUZZ TURNS NEGATIVE

Many company executives and public relations people trace their worries about social media to their belief that "people will say bad things about our company." This fear leads them to ignore blogs and online forums and to prohibit employees from participating in social media. In every discussion that I've had with employees who freely participate in social media, I've confirmed that this fear is significantly overblown. Sure, an occasional employee might vent frustrations online, and now and then a dissatisfied customer might complain. But the benefit of this kind of communication is that you can monitor in real time what's being said and then respond appropriately. Employees, customers, and other stakeholders are talking about your organization offline anyway, so unless you are participating *online*, you'll never know what's being said at all. The beauty of the Web is that you benefit from instant access to conversations you could never participate in before.

Yes, people will talk. And sometimes they might say something negative. But if you jump in and join the discussion, speaking like a human (and not a corporate automaton), you can frequently turn negative comments into positive feelings among those who read your contributions. These people will know that you and your organization care. However, when they're saying bad things about you and your products and you *don't* jump in and respond, you're flirting with disaster in the form of a World Wide *Rant*.

US AIRWAYS: COFFEE, TEA, OR A CREDIT CARD APPLICATION?

In September 2007, I published a blog post called "US Airways flight attendants paid $50 commissions to interrupt us in flight,"[69] describing a flight I'd taken from Phoenix to Boston. I was amazed and annoyed that about 90 minutes prior to landing, while most of the passengers were napping, quietly reading, or listening to music on their iPods, the cabin lights came up and a loudspeaker announcement interrupted everyone. I was jarred from sleep, as were dozens of other people.

What was so important? No, it wasn't a safety issue or other critical announcement, which I would have totally understood. Let me paraphrase what US Airways deemed more important than their customers' enjoyment of the flight: "Ladies and Gentlemen, I have great news for everyone flying with us today. You qualify for a free trip anywhere US Airways flies just by applying for the US Airways Signature Visa Card . . ." As dazed passengers rubbed their eyes, the loudspeaker barrage continued; the whole vibe of the plane changed from mellow to enraged as a flight attendant ran down a point-by-point explanation of card benefits. And then, just to make certain that everyone was fully awake, the attendant passed through the aisles, talking up the Visa card and handing out applications.

I took an application and noticed the flight attendant's name and employee ID number was already filled in. Why so much effort at interruption? After a little research on the Web, I learned that flight attendants make a $50 commission for each successful credit card sale.

[69] www.webinknow.com/2007/09/us-airways-flig.html

My blog post asked these questions: "Why do these companies deem it important to annoy their existing customers, who are the best prospects they have for repeat business? Why do these companies insult our intelligence? Do they think that loud, unwelcome marketing messages are good for their brand? Or is some rogue marketing genius doing something that the CEO and the head of customer support don't know about? Or is it just me who is annoyed and other people like this stuff?"

It wasn't just me, but more on that in a second.

I really wanted a human from US Airways to comment on my blog and explain a little about the practice that so annoyed their customers. Had someone from the company been monitoring blogs, using one of the blog search engines such as Technorati, IceRocket, or Google Blog Search, they could have known within moments that I had written about a bad experience with their service. To make certain they saw the post, I even emailed a link to representatives of their PR team.

I didn't hear a thing from US Airways.

By ignoring my blog post, the corporate communications team at US Airways perpetuated a World Wide Rant: the result of people spreading negative ideas about you, your company, and your products. I received many emails from my readers and a dozen comments on my blog. Other bloggers wrote about it, too, generating more comments on their own blogs and spreading the negativity still further. Based on my Web stats, I'd estimate that more than 20,000 people were exposed to my World Wide Rant. If US Airways had just taken ten minutes to comment, they'd have been able to humanize their company to 20,000 people. Just ten minutes' work! How difficult is that?

PARTICIPATING IN SOCIAL MEDIA

Contrast the US Airways approach with that of Harvard Business School Publishing. In May 2008, I blogged, "Does Harvard Business School know what a blog is?"[70] In this post, I wrote about an open job at Harvard Business School Publishing (HBSP), a not-for-profit, wholly owned subsidiary of Harvard University responsible for publications such as the *Harvard Business Review* magazine. The HBSP position was advertised on craigslist as "Freelance Blog Editor."

My blog post picked apart the job description: "This assistant-editor level role will serve as the principal proofreader of Harvard Business blog content. He or she will also embed appropriate internal and external links, add graphics as appropriate, format blog content for maximum readability, and suggest headlines. The assistant editor will work closely with internal Harvard Business editors and producers and occasionally with authors."

I told my readers that Harvard's idea of what a blog is was apparently very different from mine. In my opinion, the best blogs present the unfiltered opinions of people who are passionate about a topic. As soon as an editor has the role of working on Harvard Business blog content as a "proofreader," as well as by "embedding appropriate links" and "suggesting headlines," the genre of the publication changes. I think when an editor gets in the middle of an author and corporate content, you're talking propaganda. Yes, it's online content—and, yes, it is still valuable. However, in my opinion, it's just not a blog.

I asked my readers what they thought: "Am I reading too much into this?" The approach I took with the HBSP post was practically identical to the US Airways one.

[70] www.webinknow.com/2008/05/does-harvard-bu.html

I was thrilled that, on the same day I posted, Paul Michelman commented on my blog. Michelman is the director of content for Harvard Business Digital. Unlike the corporate communications people at US Airways, who ignored me, he engaged my argument, speaking directly to me and my thousands of readers.

"You make some great points—thank you for that," Michelman wrote. "The bulk of our 'blog' content is indeed more akin to the traditional column model than actual blogging." He explained how Harvard Business Digital treats blogs and its bloggers. He went on to say, "Most of our contributors post directly to the site without any editorial intervention. I can assure you that we don't see blogging as 'just the thing to do.' The future of our site is built on the notion that we need to extend our notion of participant-centered learning to the Web, and it's a terrific time to bring the community deeper into our content creation. Blogs are a critical long-term part of that strategy." Michelman concluded his comments with a preview of some new initiatives and even invited my readers to contact him.

Over the next several days, more than 20 comments appeared on my post, some of them citing Michelman and his comment. Other bloggers added to the discussions by creating posts of their own.

Clearly, Michelman was monitoring the blogosphere; he found my post in a hurry. He then took the time to write a thoughtful comment, and the tone and focus of the comments on my blog changed accordingly. Everyone participating in the discussion seemed aware that the subject of my post was also part of the conversation. By jumping in quickly, Michelman significantly added to these discussions and prevented what could have become a World Wide Rant, had many others written about Harvard and their seemingly misguided blogging policies.

I've used these two examples from my own blog for a reason. Because I originated the posts and was able to track the spread of the ideas myself, it was much easier for me to compare the tone and scope of the discussions. But the good and the bad of paying attention to social media plays out every day on countless blogs and social media sites around the world. Many smart organizations monitor blogs, forums, chat rooms, and social networking sites like Facebook and Twitter. At B&H Photo-Video,[71] Henry Posner, director of corporate communications, participates in social media discussions every day. Scott Monty,[72] digital communications executive at Ford does too. So does Ginevra Whalen, TypePad community manager at Six Apart.

PREVENTING A WORLD WIDE RANT

Blogs, forums, chat rooms, and other forms of social media are the bars, pubs, and saloons of the virtual Web community. Just like their physical counterparts, these sites bring people together to share ideas, meet friends, and gossip. And just like at your corner tavern, there are creative and intelligent people, some genuinely kind and caring folks, a few busybodies, and a smarty-pants or two. When you frequent the local bar, all these people get to know you, and you, them. You develop a reputation. If it's a good one, your friends will defend you in times of need; if it's a bad one, they'll jump on the trash-talking bandwagon. But even if you've never been to the bar before, you'll likely be given a chance to speak. The exact same opportunities exist online.

[71] www.bhphotovideo.com/
[72] http://twitter.com//scottmonty

To prevent a World Wide Rant, just be human: participate, interact, and be part of the online discussion.

Where organizations get into trouble is in failing to participate at all. If the entire village is talking about you and you stay holed up at home and never speak a word, people assume the worst.

HOW TO MONITOR AND PARTICIPATE IN SOCIAL MEDIA

Here are some ideas for monitoring blogs and other social media sites and developing a commenting strategy:

- **Participate.** Your reputation depends on it. And you may trigger a World Wide Rave or prevent a World Wide Rant.
- **Discover.** Use blog search engines like Technorati and IceRocket, general search engines like Google and Yahoo, and specialized search engines like Twitter Search[73] and the YouTube search feature to find out what people are saying.
- **Get alerts.** Set up alerts in the search engines for important phrases in your industry, region, and market. Be absolutely sure to monitor your company name and the CEO's name, as well as the names of your products and services.
- **Know the influencers.** Figure out who are the important bloggers in your industry and your market. Read the influential blogs and forums regularly so you know what people are passionate about.
- **Be truthful.** Leave comments and add to discussions—using your real name, contact information, company affiliation, and URL.

[73] http://search.twitter.com/

- **Anticipate.** Begin commenting on important blogs and forums now, before there is an issue about your organization that you need to clarify. It will improve your credibility if and when the conversation goes south.
- **Don't sell.** Never pitch your products or services on social media sites.
- **Move quickly.** If you encounter a fledgling World Wide Rant, react quickly to the discussion to humanize your company, provide relevant information, and set the record straight.
- **Be human.** People want to do business with real people. Be honest and open. Don't hide.

YOUR CHALLENGE: If you're not doing it already, begin monitoring blogs, chat rooms, forums, and social networking sites for discussions about your company and its products. Set up alerts in Google and other search engines so you'll be informed immediately when you are mentioned in the blogosphere. Participate in the discussions that are already ongoing about you.

So, you've read this far in the book. Thanks! Obviously you're curious about what your own World Wide Rave should look like. That's terrific. For now, remember that the first step in answering that question is to stop worrying and stop making excuses. Jump in and join. Have fun with it. And be creative. As Nylander's and Jackson's experiments show, and the Cities I've Visited application drives home, it's possible to make anything into a World Wide Rave if you can capture the attention of a community on the Web.

CREATE TRIGGERS THAT ENCOURAGE PEOPLE TO SHARE

NOTHING IS GUARANTEED
TO BE A WORLD WIDE RAVE

There are people who will tell you that it is possible to create an online campaign that will certainly be a hit. These hucksters are generally from viral marketing agencies that seem to specialize only in taking money and making promises. In truth, I've noticed that when they set out to create buzz, the vast majority of their campaigns fail.

It is virtually impossible to create a Web marketing program that is *guaranteed* to become a World Wide Rave; it requires a huge amount of luck and timing. That's an important point to remember as you work on your marketing ideas, because it's unlike the old-rules, numbers-based marketing techniques you're probably used to. Consider a direct-mail campaign: You could always count on a direct-mail piece to generate a known response rate, say 2 percent. So if you needed to have 100 people respond, you sent out 5,000 mailers. Easy, right?

Marketing by getting others to tell your story for you is much different. You just can't count on numbers in the same way. Many efforts fail miserably, and there are countless web sites, e-books, and videos that only their creators' mothers and bosses have seen. However, tomorrow those same marketers might be lucky enough to get a million people to view their content, driving tens of thousands of people's interest in their products and services.

However, this importance of timing and luck shouldn't discourage you from using viral marketing techniques; you just need to learn how to turn the odds in your favor.

THINK LIKE A VENTURE CAPITALIST

The best way to begin a marketing initiative that has the potential to go viral and become a World Wide Rave is to think like a venture capitalist or film producer. While I believe it is difficult to purposely create a World Wide Rave, it is certainly possible, and the best strategy is to emulate the way venture capitalists (VCs) invest in start-up companies and studios create films. A typical VC follows a maxim stating that most ventures will fail, a few might do okay, and—hopefully—one will take off and become a large enterprise that will repay investors many times their initial investment. Record companies, book publishers, and movie studios follow the same principles, expecting that most of the projects they green-light will have meager sales but that the one hit will more than repay the cost of a bunch of flops.

The problem is that nobody knows with certainty which movie or venture-backed company in the portfolio will succeed, so finding a success is a numbers game requiring investment in many prospects. The same goes for creating a World Wide Rave.

To gain some additional insight into how VCs think (so we can apply their theories to the creation of a World Wide Rave), I spoke at length with Chris Greendale, a general partner at Kodiak Venture Partners,[74] a VC firm investing in seed and early-stage technology companies. Greendale and I are both on the board of directors of Kadient,[75] a Kodiak-funded company that provides salespeople with the information tools they need to close deals. Before working with Kodiak, Greendale was a founder of Cambridge Technology Partners and an early investor in Siebel Systems.

[74] www.kodiakvp.com/
[75] www.kadient.com/

"Putting a film together is no different than investing in a company," Greendale says. "It is a roll of the dice. With a film, you start with a good script. I'm like a producer, and I get a lot of scripts in the form of business plans. I look at the quality of the value proposition, the go-to-market strategy, and the quality of the individual. I probably see 200 deals a year, which is about one each working day, and I'll likely do only two deals a year. So that means only one in a hundred gets funded. If you look at our size fund, which is $300 million, we look to invest $8–10 million per company, all in."

Thus, if we apply our venture capital/World Wide Rave analogy, we might suppose that one needs to think of hundreds of ideas and then choose a handful to "fund" (i.e., actually create). I've worked with organizations that have done just that, thinking up literally hundreds of ideas for a potential World Wide Rave over the course of a day's brainstorming session. That's great! You never really know which one is likely to succeed, so the more good ideas, the better

To minimize poisonous internal groupthink, invite people from outside your organization to help. Teenagers and college students are especially tuned in to Internet trends and phenomena that are likely to catch fire, so you might want to recruit some to help you come up with ideas. For example, when I first got involved with Facebook, my teenage daughter made sure I didn't look like a dork online and encouraged my participation. Now, my Facebook friends share my ideas with *their* friends and colleagues to help me meet new people online.

Once Greendale funds a company and it becomes part of the Kodiak portfolio, he uses a simple rule of thumb to monitor performance.

"There is a bell curve, and we are constantly managing our portfolio on a weekly basis based on that," Greendale says. "We look at each company based on three 'buckets': We expect that, out of ten companies, three will be winners that we can sell for a profit or that might even go public, three are companies where we will only get our money back but no profit, and four are companies where we end up just flushing our money down the toilet."

THE VENTURE CAPITAL | WORLD WIDE RAVE BELL CURVE

FLUSHING MONEY
DOWN THE TOILET

JUST GETTING
YOUR MONEY BACK

THE STAR

You should think of creating a World Wide Rave in much the same way. Many attempts will be duds that won't spark any interest; a few will generate some notice and basically pay back your investment of the time required to create them; and a handful will spread to thousands or even millions of people and make the entire program of 10 or 20 initiatives worthwhile.

It's important to note what Greendale does once he and his partners have identified which bucket an investment falls into.

"When an investment is bad, we try to sell the deadbeat company for even pennies on a dollar," he says. "We want to get out in these cases because we don't want to waste money and time." The same should be true for a campaign you hoped would become a World Wide Rave but didn't. Just walk away from the effort and learn from it rather than trying to force on more and more people a campaign that doesn't resonate.

On the other hand, Greendale calls the right side the star column. "We put a great deal of money and energy into this category," he says. "When it is going great and going toward an IPO [initial public offering], we give it all of the resources that we can." You should, too! When a campaign starts to take off and spread on the Web, give it all the care and attention you can, in order to turn it into a World Wide Rave.

TRIGGERSTORM:
IDEAS FOR TRIGGERING A WORLD WIDE RAVE

A World Wide Rave can be triggered by all sorts of content on the Web. Sure, being funny or outrageous works, but as we've seen numerous times, so does simply offering valuable information. We've already looked at examples of a World Wide Rave triggered by such things as videos on YouTube (IBM's *The Art of the Sale*), e-books (Steve Chazin's *Marketing Apple* and Dr. Helaine Smith's *Healthy Mouth, Healthy Sex!*), letting influential bloggers in on a secret first (The Wizarding World of Harry Potter at Universal Orlando Resort), getting teenage girls and young women to share video clips from their mobile phones (Girls Fight Back!), creating a Facebook application (Cities I've Visited from TripAdvisor), and much more.

The best triggers are often the most imaginative. If everyone is doing videos, maybe an interactive tool is best. Having difficulty getting noticed? Maybe play off the latest headlines in the news somehow. I'll say it again: You can create a World Wide Rave, too!

Let's take a look at some other fascinating examples of a World Wide Rave triggered by online content.

GRADE YOUR WEB SITE

HubSpot,[76] provider of an inbound marketing system that small businesses use to leverage search engines, get found by more prospects, and then convert a higher percentage of prospects into customers, created the nifty Website Grader[77] as a free diagnostic tool to measure the marketing effectiveness of any web site. The tool has spread through a World Wide Rave to their target customers, including marketing professionals, Web designers, and business owners interested in improving their Internet marketing. These people see tremendous value in learning how successful their site is at attracting visitors.

The free Website Grader tool helps identify companies in need of HubSpot's paid services by drawing those companies to the HubSpot site. Plus, after using the tool, many users of Website Grader conclude on their own that they need help improving their Web marketing.

[76] www.hubspot.com/
[77] www.websitegrader.com/

"We wanted a tool that would help us figure out if a company was a good fit for the product we sell, and hopefully would actually attract people to the tool to let them self-select by running a report on their own web site," says Dharmesh Shah, founder and chief software architect at HubSpot. "We thought that if we built a valuable enough tool it would generate a lot of viral traffic, helping us to grow our business."

To get people talking about Website Grader online, Shah and his colleagues at HubSpot promoted the free tool on the popular HubSpot blog[78] and then triggered interest in the blogosphere and social media sites to drive a World Wide Rave. The team posted messages in discussion forums, submitted the site to social media web sites like Delicious and StumbleUpon, and commented on other people's blogs with a link recommending Website Grader as a valuable tool people might like to try.

The success of the Website Grader tool has been staggering. HubSpot launched Website Grader on February 23, 2007, and in a year and a half, over 500,000 unique URLs were submitted for grading. The tool was featured in a *PC magazine* article as one of the Top 100 Undiscovered Websites, and A-list bloggers such as Guy Kawasaki have written about it.

What makes this World Wide Rave particularly interesting is that the success has come from a tool that cost virtually nothing to create and to promote. "Our salespeople use a Website Grader report in every deal they work on, as a diagnostic tool to review with the prospect," says Shah. "That [report] then shows how HubSpot software, our paid product, can help them with Internet marketing. Therefore, even when it is not the original lead source, it is a valuable tool for closing a lot of other business."

The real proof of Website Grader's success comes from the amount of new business it has created. "We've closed deals with over a hundred new customers to date as a result of the Website Grader," Shah says. "That represents about $1 million in customer lifetime value. We've also produced a ton more sales opportunities currently in our pipeline, with a potential customer lifetime value of another $1 million if we close them all."

Advice for generating a World Wide Rave

from Dharmesh Shah, founder and chief software architect, HubSpot

"People love tools that provide a grade or comparison and the potential for competition. Anything that has an evaluation in it and a way to compare yourself to others has a great chance to be a success. You first get your own score, and then naturally you email your friends to compare scores with them."

. . . .

A TOOL FOR SPREADING YOUR IDEAS

As HubSpot has shown, sometimes the best form of online content to spread your ideas far and wide is an interactive tool. Like the other techniques in this book, they must be totally free. For instance, nonprofits such as CARE USA mobilize constituents to support the fight against global poverty through an email tool on the CARE web site. Members use the tool to contact government leaders about particular topics, bills, or other issues. In the world of health and fitness, Sharp HealthCare, San Diego's leading healthcare system, provides several useful tools and calculators, including one to determine whether someone's drinking habits indicate an alcohol problem and one to calculate body mass index (BMI), the standard measure for determining healthy (and unhealthy) weight ranges for a given height.

WHAT HAIRSTYLE IS BEST FOR YOU?

Another example of an interactive tool for generating a World Wide Rave comes from TheHairStyler.com,[79] a Sydney, Australia–based company that offers a virtual hairstyling tool. Members upload their photo (or use a model's) and try their choices from thousands of hairstyles and dozens of colors. The tool has a range of different hairstyle categories for both women and men, allowing people to "try" a new hairstyle without actually going to the salon. There's also a bunch of celebrities' hairstyles available, so you can see how the hot 'do of the day looks on your virtual self. Once you decide on your new look, you can print out the style and take it with you to your favorite salon. The company offers a free test drive of

[79] www.thehairstyler.com/

the tool and makes money through membership programs where consumers join so they can tweak their hairstyles regularly.

"Building specific content is better than just guessing what our members want," says Roy Caccamo, marketing manager at TheHairStyler.com. "We understand our visitors before we build an effective content strategy to reach them, building relationships that lead back to sales on our site."

The tool is another certified World Wide Rave. As of this writing, The HairStyler.com has more than 300,000 members. In addition, more than 350 salons offer the virtual hairstyling system to their clients through an online affiliate program. Proving that a World Wide Rave can introduce your products and services to a global audience, Australia-based TheHairStyler.com has affiliates in 20 countries. Just those countries beginning with the letter "C" include Canada, Colombia, Croatia, Cyprus, and the Czech Republic.

YOUR CHALLENGE: An interactive tool is frequently the perfect device for generating a World Wide Rave. Consider your own business and your expertise and then devise a clever interactive tool of your own.

WHEN YOUR PRODUCT ITSELF IS YOUR TRIGGER

Remember the first time you got a free Web-based email address? Perhaps it was Hotmail, a free product that was introduced in 1996. Or maybe you recall getting a Yahoo! Mail or Gmail account (or if you're like me, you have all three!). Do you recall how you first heard of the

Web email provider? It was most likely from a friend, colleague, or family member who sent you an email and raved about the new (and free) email address they were using. Hundreds of millions of people were exposed to Hotmail (now owned by Microsoft), Yahoo! Mail, and Gmail (from Google), and many signed up for accounts themselves.

What's so fascinating about this kind of World Wide Rave is that the product itself spreads online as people use it and share it with their online networks. Another example is Pando,[80] free peer-to-peer software that makes downloading, streaming, and sharing large media files fast and easy. People use it when they need to send a file that is too large to email as an attachment. And it spreads just like the Web email applications did—one person using Pando to send a file exposes the recipient to the application, and many who find out about it this way will then begin using it, too. Since the product launched in the summer of 2006, over 20 million people in over 150 countries have installed Pando, another World Wide Rave with a product that sells itself.

RATE YOUR INTERNSHIP EXPERIENCE

Can I guess what you're thinking? At this stage, after hearing about the online products that became a World Wide Rave, products like Pando, Gmail, and Hotmail, you might be saying, "Yeah, but I don't work for a big company with tons of resources like Google or Microsoft. How can I create a product online that sells itself?" Good question. To get some answers, I asked two young women who've done it.

[80] www.pando.com/

Lauren Grunstein and Stephanie Gurtman, both juniors at Boston University College of Communications, are co-founders of InternshipRatings.com,[81] a place for students to reveal and critique the internship world so other potential interns can get the real deal at potential employers.

"We met our freshman year in the College of Communications class," Gurtman says. "We're both career-focused and wanted to work at internships. I found an internship at a small public relations and advertising firm and Lauren was hired to do public relations for a fashion designer in New York City. Then I learned that my boss was fired three weeks prior to the start of the internship, so I was disappointed. But Lauren was really excited about a dream job. We thought for sure that Lauren's experience would be amazing and mine wouldn't, but we were wrong. It turned out differently than we thought. I ended up taking on the job of the person who was fired. I wrote press releases, I went to important meetings, and I came up with PR plans for clients. Lauren, on the other hand, was given menial tasks, like packing boxes, that were not in the job description."

When the two young women spoke during the summer, they realized that if there had been information about the companies where they were slated to intern, their experiences might have been different.

"So we decided to create a site," Grunstein says. "We are used to these kinds of user-driven ratings services because we used RateMyProfessors.com[82] a lot." RateMyProfessors.com currently has 6 million opinions on a million professors who teach at over 6,000 schools. "We saw the opportunity and we created something that we would use ourselves, with a young feel to the site as well as the company name and tagline: *Is it worth the coffee?*"

[81] www.internshipratings.com/
[82] www.ratemyprofessors.com/

Grunstein and Gurtman (who collectively call themselves "The Gigi Girls" because of the first letter of their last names) knew that the product itself was the best marketing tool. "Internships are becoming increasingly important," Gurtman says. "Many colleges are making them requirements for graduation. And ratings sites are really popular now, so we combined those two trends." They knew that as ratings were added to the site, more visitors would come and then more ratings would appear and on and on into a World Wide Rave.

To launch InternshipRatings.com, the Gigi Girls focused their efforts on social media sites. "We sent out personal messages to about a thousand of our Facebook friends," Grunstein says. "We made the messages really short and personal and told people about the site and our InternshipRatings.com Facebook group.[83] We used our network in a way where we were letting our friends into our lives. Facebook is how people of our generation communicate, so that's how we launched."

"We told people that the first phase was to build the profiles in the site," Gurtman adds. "We said that we wanted their help to build out the initial profiles."

Considering the Gigi Girls are both college students and InternshipRatings.com is a part-time project, I wondered about their career aspirations. "Our long-term goal is to pursue this full-time," Gurtman says. "It is our career path for now, but we are not going to leave school to pursue this. We see so much potential and we're eager to see results quickly."

"We feel that company internships will improve when people see that they are being rated," adds Grunstein. "The site will help to increase the experience for all internship programs."

[83] www.facebook.com/group.php?gid=9989149988

BE FIRST AND BE FAST

Sometimes, the best way to start a World Wide Rave is to piggyback off of another, much larger one. For example, when the iPhone was released, it generated a huge World Wide Rave. People were talking about the iPhone constantly, online and off. Into that fray stepped many companies and individuals who started to create applications for the iPhone. Those started to be talked about as well, and some generated World Wide Raves of their own.

A great example of an iPhone application that was available on the release day of the new iPhone 3G model on July 11, 2008, comes from Tapulous,[84] producers of *Tap Tap Revenge*. This application immediately became the Number 1 free game on the iPhone. How about this for a World Wide Rave spreading like wildfire: *Tap Tap Revenge* was downloaded by 200,000 people in just the first three days of availability. On the second day of its availability, 25,000 people entered a *Tap Tap Revenge* tournament. Within a month they had reached one million users. Wow. What an amazing success.

I had an opportunity to visit with Tapulous founders and investors in their Palo Alto, CA headquarters just four days after the launch of the application. Robert Scoble, who writes the scobleizer blog[85] and is managing director of FastCompany.TV,[86] invited me to tag along as he filmed a video with the company founders and investors. Besides the amazing success of the game, what I found fascinating is when Andrew Lacy, Tapulous's COO, talked about adding exclusive new music tracks to the *Tap Tap Revenge* game soundtrack. The music industry has come a long way. You used to have to go to traditional publishers to get music out there. Then MySpace was a way to self-publish music. Now a game application—downloaded by over a million people in a month—is a new way for an indie band to earn some big-time notice.

Another company that was quick out of the gate with an iPhone application is SpeakerCraft,[87] a maker of architectural speaker systems used in homes and commercial settings. SpeakerCraft created an application that transforms an iPhone into a remote control unit that can be used to access a home theater and multiroom audio system. You walk through the front door of your house, reach into your pocket, and with your iPhone start playing your favorite tunes from your home audio system. The SpeakerCraft interface works like other iPhone applications, so its operation is intuitive. Your play list, artist names, and songs are all displayed on your iPhone together with volume and other controls.

Since SpeakerCraft was among the first companies to offer this interesting way to use an iPhone, many bloggers and gadget sites covered the product release. As of this writing, there are over 10,000 hits on Google for the combination of words "SpeakerCraft" and "iPhone." The company's newest product got a huge push from iPhone enthusiasts, resulting in a World Wide Rave.

Sometimes, just being the first product out of the gate, or the first to exploit a new technology or change in regulations, can lead to success.

YOUR CHALLENGE: Create a team and a process in advance and get internal preapprovals in place so that when a new trend breaks, you can respond very quickly. If you work for a nimble organization, an instant response to something in the news, a reaction to a change in regulations, or a clever piggyback off somebody else's World Wide Rave can be both fun and rewarding.

A WORLDWIDE VIRTUAL EVENT

Most people agree that one of the coolest things about the Web is the ease with which you can bring together people from all over the world. I'm amazed that the readers of my blog come from dozens of countries, and I often get comments from many of them. But it's even cooler when people come together for a shared experience in real time. Sometimes, a great way to trigger a World Wide Rave is to stage some kind of virtual event, like a simple Web-based seminar (Webinar) or an entire virtual conference.

Krishna De,[88] a brand engagement strategist based in Dublin, Ireland, is part of a network of experts who advise people about personal branding. De and several others in her network recognized that it had been ten years since the phrase "A brand called You" was used in a groundbreaking *Fast Company* magazine article by Tom Peters,[89] so they hit upon the idea of celebrating the milestone in some way that would help people understand the ideas of personal branding.

"We decided to recognize the tenth anniversary of personal branding with a virtual event called the Personal Branding Summit," De says. "And we wanted to make it a global program. Because it was global, we tried to find a date six months ahead that wasn't on a holiday in any

[88] www.krishnade.com/blog/
[89] www.fastcompany.com/magazine/10/brandyou.html

of the major countries of the world where we would draw attendees, that wasn't near any elections, [and that didn't have] any other issues. We settled on November 8, 2007."

De, who served as chair of the Personal Branding Summit,[90] pulled together a team of volunteers to organize the event. A critical first task was recruiting speakers. "We wanted to bring together a team of people who would be strategic," De says. "We wanted speakers who were authors. And we wanted to cover the spectrum of personal branding, including things like resume writing, career management, and entrepreneurship. And we wanted people to work with us as a community and promote their participation for us, so we chose people who had blogs. We chose to make it a free event, so we couldn't pay the speakers. Anyone who was a significant blogger understood immediately that it was a benefit to be associated with the event, and many agreed to participate."

The really remarkable part? "None of us who worked on it had ever met in person," De says. "We came together as a virtual event."

Continuing to emphasize the global aspect of the event, the team chose to create 24 hours of continuous programming. That way, no matter where potential participants lived, they could listen in during a convenient time. "The biggest expense was the telecommunications cost," De says. "Conference Calls Unlimited[91] came in as a Gold Sponsor and covered all of the live telecommunications costs and also recorded all the calls and made them available as a podcast. And we wanted to give back to the global community, so we partnered with Kiva[92] as our charity to promote during the event. At the start of every call, we promoted Kiva [the world's first person-to-person microlending

[90] www.personalbrandingsummit.com/
[91] www.conferencecallsunlimited.com/
[92] www.kiva.org/

web site that connects individuals to lend directly to entrepreneurs in the developing world] with an announcement to donate."

I was fortunate to be one of several dozen presenters at the Personal Branding Summit along with Dick Bolles, America's top career expert and author of the best-selling career and job-hunting guide in the world (*What Color Is Your Parachute?*, which has sold over nine million copies); Debbie Weil, author of the *Corporate Blogging Book*; Andy Sernovitz, author of *Word of Mouth Marketing*; Guy Kawasaki , venture capitalist and author of *The Art of the Start*; John Jantsch, creator of the Duct Tape Marketing method, and many others.

The main vehicle for promotion was the millions of collective readers of the presenters' blogs, podcasts, newsletters, and other online communications programs. In effect, the presenters did the marketing for the event. "We directly connected to the blogging community," De says. "Some of the sponsors had newsletters and email footers and we had many mentions in podcasts and in peoples' live speeches. We also talked about the event on Twitter, Facebook, and other social media."

Like all the other presenters, I blogged about my participation.[93] In fact, the blog promotions were so critical to the event's success that the organizers decided to use a blog, instead of a traditional web site, as its official promotional vehicle. "We used a blog platform so we could have links and comments on the official event pages," De says. "We gave people who were speaking the chance to post articles onto the blog. We really used the blog as a community and recorded some podcast interviews to promote it and it was a fantastic success."

---

[93] www.webinknow.com/2007/10/a-brand-your-wo.html

The Personal Branding Summit was a hit with thousands of people from all over the world sitting in on the virtual presentations. "We had tons of coverage from bloggers with a flurry of conversations, so we knew we were getting reach prior to the event itself. We've been able to deliver great content to people from across the globe on the subject of personal branding," De says. She estimates that listeners heard over 200,000 hours of information. "We also know which areas were of the most interest to our listeners, which helps us plan the next event. And the shows in the meantime continue to be downloaded from the web site and through iTunes—all while we are sleeping!"

AN AEROSPACE LECTURE AT THE GYM

Most people working in small marketing teams at little-known universities far from major cities don't even try to compete with the huge, famous, and rich universities around the world. They just invest in traditional advertising and marketing techniques, like sending fancy direct mail to every high school junior in the area with good grades, in order to tell the institution's story and attempt to drive admissions.

That's not what Donald Kojich, executive associate vice president for university relations at the University of North Dakota (UND)[94] did. UND enrolls more than 12,000 students in nearly 200 fields of study from bachelor's through doctoral and professional degrees. With about half of the students coming from outside North Dakota, including students from more than 50 nations, Kojich's job of getting the word out is a challenge.

"When I started at UND, I wanted to find ways to use technology to tell our story," he says. "I am big into anything to take advantage of Web 2.0

[94] www.webinknow.com/2007/10/a-brand-your-wo.html

to push out our content. At the time, Apple had just created a new environment called iTunes University[95] [also called iTunes U] where institutions could put up podcasts [later it was expanded to include video]. This is a place that we put information to make it easy for students, potential students, and alumni donors to download and learn more about what we do here at UND."

Apple created iTunes U in collaboration with colleges and universities that were looking for ways to expand and enrich their curricula with digital content. Like everything in iTunes, the course content can be played on a computer or synched to an iPod to allow students to learn whenever and wherever they want. For instance, some use it to listen to language lessons at the gym or to review lectures on the bus.

"The UND Aerospace Program is well known, and we wanted a way to drive people to our institution," says Kojich. "Putting audio onto iTunes U was a way for us to create a stronger presence. The UND aerospace program had been doing podcasts for about a year prior to that, so we worked with them and other academic units on content development." This UND aerospace content is called AeroCast[96] on iTunes U.

Kojich faced initial resistance from colleagues in the UND faculty and administration. "We had a vision for what this could do, but the concept was foreign to many academics," he says. "So we had to educate people at the institution about how to use audio content. I told my colleagues: 'This is a great way that you can use content to tell your story in a different fashion.'"

Once Kojich got the go-ahead, creating the content and uploading it to iTunes U was simple. "With technology like this, you don't need to have

---

[95] www.apple.com/education/itunesu_mobilelearning/itunesu.html
[96] www2.und.edu/our/itunes/index.php

high-end production value," he says. "Five years ago, you needed studio space and you had to spend thousands to produce high-end information and put it on a CD and deal with distribution. We recorded faculty lecture series and put them onto the iTunes U. This is a great way to communicate to anyone anywhere in the world who has interest in a particular subject."

Soon the aerospace content was enhanced with podcasts from other departments, including the UND medical school's MedCast and information for prospective students from the admissions office.

The efforts have proven beneficial. "When we launched, we generated a lot of statewide media coverage," Kojich says. And the availability of aerospace content to anyone in the world drives admissions. "We know that some prospective students first found out about the aerospace program via podcasts. These are students who wouldn't have applied to UND otherwise."

How about that? A World Wide Rave via faculty lectures.

Advice for generating a World Wide Rave

from Donald Kojich, executive associate vice president for university relations
at the University of North Dakota

"You don't have to be top-of-mind with a famous name to get awareness. Even a smaller or less well known institution can get more visibility and raise the platform of your institution. We looked at many different ways to tell our story, but with audio and video it is much more interactive. You can push out your message and target it better. Part of the benefit is also the metrics. You can measure how many people go to each URL and measure the traffic. In our case, it has taken off."

. . . .

CREATE A CONTEST, YOU MIGHT TRIGGER A RAVE

When people are interacting with you by leaving comments or creating original content, it shows the world that people care. Sometimes, a great way to jumpstart user-generated content efforts is to hold a contest. This can be tricky to pull off, because you want to be seen as authentic and interesting. Don't let your contest come across as overly forced.

A great example of a contest done well is "Supe-up your Ride," which was created through a partnership between Barbican,[97] a drink popular with young people in the Middle East, and Maktoob Clipat,[98] the Arab world's premier video-sharing portal.

Barbican and Maktoob identified car customization as important to its buyer personas, young Arab men. The Supe-up your Ride promotion offered consumers the chance to win a free car customization and used online video as the submission mechanism. Contestants simply uploaded short videos of their cars to illustrate why they needed to get the makeover (like in MTV's popular *Pimp My Ride* show). Over 1,800 people across the Gulf region sent in their videos. During the three-month contest period, submissions were received from the Kingdom of

[97] www.aujan.com/home/aujan.aspx?id=6
[98] http://clipat.maktoob.com/

Saudi Arabia, United Arab Emirates, Kuwait, Bahrain, Oman, and Qatar. A lucky winner was chosen each month. (The first winner, Naem Alfar, shot a video of his sad-looking minivan.[99]) Tens of thousands of consumers voted for their favorite submission online. Car makeovers were tailored to the personality and interests of the owners, and the work usually included a paint job, new accessories, chrome, tires, rims, and installation of the latest sound systems and electronics.

Those who enter contests like this are likely to tell their network of friends about their entry, both to solicit votes and to share the good news if they win. And everyone involved with the contest gets exposed to the organizers' products and services, which is the whole point, right?

YOUR CHALLENGE: Think about the kinds of user-generated content that would naturally tie in with your product, and devise an online contest of your own.

ENTER A CONTEST, YOU MIGHT WIN

For some people, the work involved in designing and executing a contest might be a little too involved. So why not enter somebody else's? If you win, your entry may be seen by thousands or even millions of people. And the work involved to enter may be surprisingly small.

Mike Lefebvre, a real estate agent with Century 21 Commonwealth in Massachusetts, was new to the business and realized that he needed to do things differently than everyone else if he was to succeed in a competitive market. "When I started in the business, it was a horrible time to get into the market. There were thousands of houses on the market and thousands of realtors."

After only a year's experience as an agent, he'd created his own web site,[100] plus a standalone web site for each property he marketed. "I make them myself," he says. "I [include] YouTube videos, audio testimonials from neighbors, tons of photos, [and] interactive Google maps, and I include an appraisal right on the site so I can be transparent about the price. Both buyers and sellers really like this."

His business took off when he created a video called "Steak Out in Franklin, MA,"[101] which highlighted one of his listings in an unconventional way. The video, shot by himself with a $150 Flip Video camera, tells the story of a mystery in the home he was marketing and features both Lefebvre and the home seller. Lefebvre entered the video in two contests and won them both. "The first contest I won in April was for ActiveRain, a social network of real estate professionals. For my prize, ActiveRain sent me to New York City for a one-day seminar with Seth Godin. And I also won the Century 21 'Dig the Digs' YouTube video contest for the most entertaining and unique video. The rules were simple: The contest was open to any Century 21 agent in the United States; both the agent and the homeowner needed to be in the video; and it had to be under two minutes. I won first prize, $21,000 and an HDTV for me. My sellers [the owner of the home in the video] also received an HDTV. I then used the photo of the Century 21 executive handing me the large phony check as a way to get local newspaper coverage in my market. On the very same day the corporate people from Century 21 were up here to present the check, the house went under agreement and recently sold."

In a short period of time, Lefebvre has become very well known in national real estate circles as a result of his video. "I expect to have the number-one

[100] www.theUncommonAgent.com
[101] http://youtube.com/watch?v=2WFV3S44Y6g

social-media-enabled real estate company in Massachusetts and to be making a lot of money. I couldn't do that any other way. I couldn't do that with cold calling and door knocking. I can only do it with social media like videos, Facebook, and Twitter. I think a lot of people in this business are lazy. They just put a sign on the yard, list it on the Multiple Listing Service System, and hope for the best. While other brokers make excuses for their poor business, I make videos and web sites and make the sale."

Soon after I spoke with Lefebvre, he contacted me to let me know that his social media efforts got the attention of Hallmark Sotheby's International Realty in Hopkinton, MA. "Hallmark Realty is an established, successful high-end boutique real estate company operating in the suburbs of Boston," Lefebvre says. "Erica Wallace at Hallmark Realty found me online through Twitter, dug a little deeper through Facebook, LinkedIn, ActiveRain, and my site, and learned about my video contest win. We started up a conversation via Twitter. Shortly thereafter I met with Erika Paul, the owner, and Erica Wallace. From the 'overused-business-cliché,' department, they simply made me an offer I couldn't refuse."

How about that? A World Wide Rave leads to landing a dream job! "With a young, progressive, raving-Internet-fans team in charge, I knew my online efforts would be supported and highly encouraged," Lefebvre says. "I just celebrated my first year in the real estate sales business. I am by no means a 'top producer' or 'star performer,' volume-wise. I was recruited based solely on my online presence and social media strategy, not for all the business I would bring through the door [on] day one. So the next time someone asks me if I ever got any direct business off Twitter, I will chime up and tell them I got one hell of a promotion off Twitter!"

YOUR CHALLENGE: Entering an online contest of some kind, perhaps one involving a video, might be just the thing to motivate you to create some compelling content. Go for it—you've got nothing to lose!

SHOWCASE YOUR CUSTOMERS

A great way to spread your ideas is to use your customers to tell your stories for you. Potential customers are eager to hear from people like them, and they pay close attention to how others have been helped by a product or service. Satisfied customers will often talk up favored companies—on forums and chat rooms, on blogs, on Facebook, and in other social network sites. These stories are so valuable that many companies encourage them and publish the examples on their sites.

USA Cares[102] (not to be confused with CARE USA or, for that matter USA for Africa) is a nonprofit organization that provides assistance to military families of U.S. service members returning home from the wars in Iraq and Afghanistan. "Two crises are affecting American families," says Roger Stradley, director of program development for USA Cares. "A large number suffer from post-traumatic stress disorder (PTSD) and traumatic brain disorder (TBI), causing significant economic hardship on their families. And due to the ongoing nationwide mortgage crisis, a large number of military families are losing their home to foreclosure, [at] almost four times the national rate in some areas." Since 2003, USA Cares has helped 11,000 military families with financial support and other resources.

[102] www.usacares.org/

The organization profiles on its web site families it has helped, both as examples of how the donations are used as well as to encourage those in need to seek support. For instance, there's the story of a 23-year Army Reserve veteran with two tours of duty in Iraq who was wounded as the tractor-trailer he was driving was hit by an IED and then came under small-arms fire. The wounds he received spelled an end to his career, and he came back home to Long Island, New York. But his Social Security and Disability benefits were inadequate to keep his mortgage current on the home he shares with his wife and 14 year-old daughter. He was facing foreclosure and also needed help to renovate the home, since his disability prevented him from climbing steps. USA Cares came through with $7,430 to save the home from foreclosure, and another national nonprofit organization, Rebuilding Together, helped with renovations to the home. Stories like this help make vivid and concrete the problems faced by military families in need. "The actual stories provide the credentials and credibility of USA Cares to those who help us with their donation," Stradley says.

In addition, the clients they help offer testimonials in what USA Cares calls their "guest book" on the USA Cares site. A family from Oceanside, Camp Pendleton, writes: "I just wanted to extend my appreciation. . . . My family was in desperate need to get our car out of repossession status and thanks to the hard work of [USA Cares] we don't have to worry about losing our car anymore. You both lifted so much stress off of our shoulders, thank you is just not enough to express our gratitude to [USA Cares]." A service member from Fort Walton Beach, Eglin Air Force Base, says: "Thanks so much to USA Cares!! With the help we received, my family was able to climb out of the hole we were digging ourselves into. They gave us just the help we needed to tie the ends together."

For visitors to the USA Cares site as well as the media and bloggers who write about the organization, these stories—in the clients' own words—are incredibly powerful. "It is very moving to have the success stories page and hear from the people we've helped," says Stradley. "At the end of the process, our clients, the military families, thank the people who helped them. A number of Army wives and Marine mothers have told me that they actually start crying as result of reading the guest book and the stories." Moving people to action is the very goal of this group, and so sharing such powerful stories is essential.

CREATIVITY AND IMAGINATION REQUIRED

The collection of ideas that I've provided here is by no means complete. I'm sure I'm missing dozens of other categories of interesting and compelling Web content that has spread ideas to thousands of people. But my goal wasn't to chronicle each and every technique. Rather, I hope that these stories spark an idea for you.

While each profiled a different way to reach people online, the unifying thing that ties them together is that somebody applied a little creativity and imagination. And that's often the only ingredient required to trigger a World Wide Rave.

POINT
THE WORLD
TO YOUR
(virtual)
DOORSTEP

YOU CAN'T TRIGGER A WORLD WIDE RAVE
IF YOU'RE INVISIBLE

People often ask me about search engine optimization. In particular, many want search engine marketing techniques they can use to "get high rankings" for their site. Almost inevitably, I find that the sites these people want optimized suck. They're poorly written. They ramble on and on in an egotistical way about what the companies' products do. They're filled with industry jargon and corporate gobbledygook.

I tell these people that they need to understand their buyers and create great content that buyers will want to consume. That way, their pages will attain high rankings as the search engine algorithms gradually reward the great content.

Usually I get pushback. People say they just want an agency to "tweak our existing Web pages."

"Sorry," I say. "The only way to create high search engine results is to create great stuff that people want to link to." And I go on to give examples of how valuable Web content drives high rankings.

 Performing search engine optimization on a crap-filled site just makes it slightly less crappy.

I'm amazed by how a piece of interesting information (a blog post, an e-book, a Web page) can generate high rankings for a tiny company, rankings way above those of the big, famous organizations.

Consider this example from my own efforts: Prior to publishing my e-book *The New Rules of Viral Marketing*, my site and blog were ranked way down on the 15-or-so Google results page for the phrase "viral marketing," an important search term for me since I write and speak about viral marketing. My stuff was something like the 120th result—Siberia when it comes to search engines, because almost nobody will dig that far down. I was nowhere. More than a hundred other sites were ranked higher than mine. However, as of this writing, because of an e-book that has become a World Wide Rave (it has been downloaded more than 250,000 times, and hundreds of bloggers have written about it), my site is now on the first page of Google results out of more than 5 million hits for this important phrase. Even I was surprised by the success—and it's what I had set out to do!

YOUR CHALLENGE: Go to Google and do a search for the important phrases that your buyers are using to find organizations like yours, and look at where you fall in the search results. Consider what great content you can publish to trigger a World Wide Rave that will get people linking to your content and send your site to the top of the search results.

#1 SEARCH RESULT ON GOOGLE

Ever wonder how a small company with limited resources gets the Number 1 search result on Google (and the other search engines) for the most important phrase to promote their business? If you've read this book from the beginning, then you can certainly guess how it's done. I'm sure by now you appreciate that you don't buy your way to Number 1. And despite what the expensive search engine marketing companies will tell you, you don't do it by tweaking your existing web site to make it "search engine friendly" (whatever that means). Tweaking bad Web content is just putting lipstick on a pig. Don't settle for bad content.

The way to actually drive search engine success is to generate some fascinating information that people want to consume, put it on the Web for free, and in the process drive a World Wide Rave right to your virtual door.

Search for the phrase "email marketing metrics" on Google and you'll find 365,000 hits plus dozens of paid advertisements. This is a hot search phrase because people who want to manage an email marketing program for their organization—small business owners, consultants, people who work in marketing departments of large organizations, and nonprofits— often search for important email marketing benchmarks (things like click-through rates and the best days of the week to begin campaigns). With so many companies fighting for the high search positions for the phrase "email marketing metrics," only one can be the top dog. Meet Mailer-Mailer, the company that controls the Number 1 position. MailerMailer sells an online tool that makes it easy to create, send, and track email campaigns. The tool is used by musicians, restaurants, software companies, event promoters, nonprofits, and other organizations. This small company is Number 1 because of its free *Email Marketing Metrics Report*.[103]

 With a well-placed article, blog post, or microsite, you can reach your buyers via search engines. It doesn't require detailed knowledge of search engine algorithms' inner workings. It simply requires knowledge of your buyers.

[103] www.mailermailer.com/metrics/

Of course, it's no surprise at all that the Number 1 spot for an important search term was garnered by a company that creates some very valuable information and offers it to anyone for free. "We analyzed over 300 million opt-in email newsletters and campaigns sent by a sample of over 3,200 MailerMailer customers in the second half of 2007," says Raj Khera, CEO of MailerMailer. "This free report reveals the most recent email marketing trends." For example, readers will discover which industries experienced the highest percentage of email opening rates and how frequently to send them to reach the most people. Chock-full of charts and graphs, the valuable data made available here for free would likely command a price of $10,000 (or more) if a consulting firm put it out.

YOUR CHALLENGE: What proprietary data and metrics do you have that would be valuable to others? Publish them and offer them for free to generate a World Wide Rave.

QUOTED ALL OVER THE WEB

The free *Email Marketing Metrics Report* has helped MailerMailer create a World Wide Rave. "Our metrics are now quoted all over the Web, in places like eMarketer and Marketing Sherpa, and by ad agencies, companies, bloggers, reporters, analysts, and others who use it for data in their stories and reports," Khera says. "We've seen over 500 blogs pointing to the data. There was a tremendous amount of industry recognition about the report."

The *Email Marketing Metrics Report* was first released October 2004. "Initially we required registration to get the report [downloaders needed to supply an email address], and we got some initial interest, but not big numbers," Khera says. "When we opened it up and made the report available totally free, we found that twenty times the number of people downloaded it. Thousands of people were getting it."

Wow, stop and think about that. Many companies put registration requirements on their most valuable content. But here is real evidence that if you do, only a fraction of potential readers or viewers will request it. As I mentioned earlier in the book, other companies have cited to me that as few as one person in 50 will download something if personal information is required, compared to when the same information is offered totally free.

Once it was clear that the report was a success, MailerMailer began updating the data and putting out a revision twice per year. In the meantime, Khera has smartly built relationships with people in a position to promote the *Email Marketing Metrics Report* online. "We saw a number of publications picking up the data, and many reporters were people that we did not know before," he says. "Now we've developed relationships with many of them as a result."

Khera also maintains ties with influential bloggers who use the report. "When people post about the metrics report, I will go in and leave an appropriate comment," he says. "And when we have a new metrics report, we release it first to a handful of important bloggers."

Clearly, having one of the most popular and most referenced sources of email marketing data is a huge marketing asset. When people read about email marketing metrics in a report from MailerMailer, they naturally consider purchasing MailerMailer products and services to help them with their email marketing programs. Right in the report is a free trial offer for MailerMailer services. "We're one of the top-ten companies in the email marketing space," says Khera. "The product promotes itself."

Advice for generating a World Wide Rave

from Raj Khera, CEO of MailerMailer

"The biggest thing we've learned is that when you have useful data, people will want to use it. It took a while for us to make sense of all of the data and to make valuable charts and graphs of the data. The first report took three person-months to produce. But the efforts were worth it. The branding that we've been able to accomplish with the report is amazing."

High search engine rankings are not created through manipulation or trickery. They are the result of offering excellent content.

To help buyers find you via search engines, answer this sequence of questions:

1. Do you know the most important search terms that people are using to find products and services like the ones you sell?
2. Where do you appear in those results?
3. Where do your competitors appear?

YOUR CHALLENGE: If you aren't satisfied with your search engine placement, consider what great content you can create (like a blog or an e-book or some news releases) to draw links from other people and help boost your ranking.

CONTROLLING THE UNCONTROLLABLE

An important aspect of creating valuable content that gets shared is choosing a great title for your YouTube video, e-book, blog post, and so on. People are much more eager to link to a catchy or controversial title. For example, one of my more popular blog posts is titled "Advertising agency web sites: Digital Masturbation."[104] People are intrigued by a title like this and they want to read more, so they click to see what's there.

Other blog post titles I've written that have generated large traffic include the following (if you want to read one, just Google the phrase):

- "For best results, stick it in the fridge"
- "Do you know this person? Is it you?"
- "8 tips to make your YouTube video go viral"
- "Branding is for cattle"
- "The Gobbledygook Manifesto"

When I write a blog post, I always want the ideas to spread online to as many people as possible. However, sometimes I just know in my gut I've got a really interesting concept that has potential to reach tens of thousands of people or more. When I feel like I'm sitting on a great idea, I think very carefully about the title of the blog post.

It's really fun to consciously create a "viral post" that will trigger a bunch of inbound links. It feels a little like loading the dice to control the uncontrollable. Part of the strategy is to know when you've got something particularly interesting, so you can focus a little extra effort on it. Sure, all your blog posts should be good, but it's impossible to make them all great. One technique I've used to signal my readers that content is especially shareable is to pose an open-ended question within the post: "What do you think?" or "Would this work for you?" That tends to get people involved, and many will write comments on my blog, responses on their blogs, or share with their network. But if you try this technique, use it sparingly; the effect wears off if you use it in every post.

DO NOT READ THIS PART OF THE BOOK

So you're reading this section, huh? Kind of an enticing subheading, isn't it? Why is that?

I have strong evidence that "negative" headlines and titles often generate a lot more clicks than "positive" ones. Why do tabloid newspapers put scandals on the cover? Because those big, fat, nasty headlines sell newspapers. Several of my blogger friends have experimented with negative headlines, with fascinating results. For example, Jonathan

Kranz, a freelance copywriter who works with companies to create marketing materials, has a link[105] on his site called "Important Reasons NOT to Hire Me." Here are some of the reasons: "You like jargon," "You want to play it safe," and "You like vague messaging." Kranz says the negative word *NOT* attracts attention.

It turns out people react to negatives. Several years ago, I worked on a site where we included a link "For Executives Only," which generated more traffic than other links. Words like *worst, not, don't,* and *only* are interesting, and people want to know what's there.

Mark R. Hinkle, VP of business and community development at IT infrastructure monitoring company Zenoss, is a popular technology futurist. Hinkle wrote a blog post titled "Top 10 Reasons Not to Use Ubuntu."[106] The post reads, "I played around with Ubuntu this weekend and I have been really impressed by everything, but I know many people still want to use a Windows desktop. So I thought I would give you 10 reasons why you shouldn't use Ubuntu so when your Ubuntu-loving friends tell you about it you can be armed with some reasons why you would rather use Windows." Two of the reasons he provides are "Installation of Software is Too Easy," and "Too Few Viruses/Too much security."

Hinkle says the reaction was amazing. The next morning he woke to find the post on the front page of Digg with more than 100 diggs. (People use Digg[107] to discover and share content from anywhere on the Web. Instead of determining important content with mathematical algorithms like a search engine or through the use of a professional editor like online news sites, Digg users identify the best content at a given moment as voted on by users—people collectively determine its value.) In the days immediately following the post, his blog got ten times the normal traffic, and the

[105] www.kranzcom.com/
[106] http://socializedsoftware.com/2007/10/30/top-10-reasons-not-to-use-ubuntu/
[107] http://digg.com/

hits keep coming. An added benefit was that he found he enjoyed writing the post from the negative viewpoint—it got his creative juices flowing.

I think what people are really saying when they vote with their mouse by clicking on negative headlines is that they crave authenticity. Again, we all want to know that the company we're researching or the blogger we're reading is human. Deluged with so many upbeat corporate messages, many site visitors don't find much authenticity out there. When a marketer uses some alternative language, particularly with negative connotations, people sit up and pay attention. And often the "negative" can trigger a World Wide Rave.

YOUR CHALLENGE: Take a look at your site and find a link you can flip around. Measure the traffic before and after the switch and see which version works better. Perhaps your site includes a headline like this: "How to increase productivity and drive revenue." *Yawn.* How many times have we all read something like that? How about this: "How to destabilize productivity, deter customers, and diminish revenue." Now that's likely to get some attention!

While the negative technique most certainly works, it also should be used sparingly so as not to diminish the effect. Usually, only one negative link on a site is appropriate. And remember—there must be something compelling and interesting to read once people click it. You need to be creative. Write something that people will find clever or funny but that will still tie back to your organization in some way. Don't promise something interesting and then fail to deliver. When people do click, the landing page should immediately signal that you're having fun. Don't be too subtle. Don't let people think that you really are being negative or exclusionary. Bring them in with the negative hook, but then let them in on the joke.

HIRE A JOURNALIST

I know that I've gone on and on about how the best way to create a World Wide Rave is to create great content and publish it online for free. I know that, for some of you, that might be easier said than done. "But if I knew how to create great content, I'd already be doing it," you might say. Earlier, I told you to think like a venture capitalist, but you also need to think like a journalist.

 One of the best ways to create great Web content is to actually hire a journalist, either full- or part-time, to create it.

Journalists, both print and broadcast, are great at understanding an audience and creating content that buyers want to consume—it's the bread-and-butter of their skill set.

At a recent speaking gig in North Carolina, I met a journalist-turned-marketer named Kathy Boyd. Boyd works in corporate communications at Neighborhood America,[108] a company that creates enterprise social networks for organizations to reach consumers. Boyd is exactly the sort of person I'm talking about. She studied mass media communications and broadcast journalism at Florida State and upon graduation spent a few years as a TV reporter for WFTX-TV, the Fox affiliate in Fort Myers, Florida.

After Boyd honed her journalism skills as a TV reporter, she joined Neighborhood America and now works on the company's corporate newsletter and produces some stellar videos, including a video case study of Adidas, a Neighborhood America client. In the video, "Adidas Goes Mobile At NBA All-Star Week 2007,"[109] viewers are treated to a

[108] www.neighborhoodamerica.com/
[109] www.youtube.com/watch?v=zj1o_nOwQus

short, punchy, and engaging example of how Adidas uses Neighborhood America's services. The video takes an approach that's utterly different from most companies. Almost inevitably, such typical case studies: (1) are dreadfully boring, (2) prattle on incessantly about the product, or (3) do both. Kudos to Neighborhood America for taking a chance on hiring a journalist to do marketing instead of taking the safe route of a traditional marketing hire.

With the consolidation of the newspaper and magazine businesses, journalists have (sadly) found it difficult to get and keep good jobs. Many experienced people are looking for work, and the number of people coming out of journalism school almost always exceeds the number of available entry-level jobs. Of course, this is a dire situation for many reporters and editors themselves but a tremendous opportunity for corporate marketing and PR departments that need to find great talent to create effective content.

Sure, Web marketing represents a dramatically different job description from, say, beat reporter, and some marketing VPs may have trouble getting their heads around this kind of hire. But I'm convinced, based on the characteristic skill set and work ethic of the journalists I know, and on evidence from companies like IBM that have already experimented with hiring journalists into the marketing department, that this approach is a good one.

Due to plain old supply-and-demand factors, journalists' salaries are—unfortunately for them—on the low side. However, I predict that as corporations learn that journalists are terrific marketing assets and they begin to hire them in larger numbers, their salaries will increase. At the same time, I think journalists need to think deeply about the opportunities that a corporate assignment might bring to their careers. Many journalists have a strong emotional aversion to "selling their skills to corporations." While some would rather wait tables than work for "the dark side," others may find the opportunity refreshing and beneficial to their careers. It may even make them more marketable for traditional gigs with publications, as long as they continue to create quality content while pioneering this new form of corporate journalism.

A note of caution here: When I recommend that you hire a journalist to create content for your site, I am not advocating the old-school *advertorial* model. Advertorials are those late-night cable TV shows about a product or the full-page product information "reports" found in trade journals. While these may be valid marketing for some organizations, the idea of using a journalist should be to educate and inform, not to overtly try to sell products. Compare Boyd's Adidas video to any handy juicer or workout tape infomercial next time you're up with a bout of insomnia and you'll see what I mean.

A good journalist can create interesting stories about how an organization solves customer problems and can then deliver those stories in a variety of forms: articles, e-books, Web content, podcasts, and video. Consumers will love it. How refreshing to read, listen to, and watch these products of journalistic expertise instead of the usual come-ons that typical corporations produce.

The Internet offers an easy way for ideas to spread instantly to a potential audience of millions of people. Web content in the form of true thought leadership—the kind that tells important, thoughtful stories— holds the potential to influence many thousands of your buyers in ways that traditional marketing and PR simply cannot. Yet harnessing the power of the Web and the blogosphere requires a different kind of thinking from marketers' usual approaches. We need to learn to give up our command-and-control mentality. It isn't about "the message." It's about being insightful. We need to reconsider our dependence on advertising and instead get our ideas out there by understanding buyers and telling them the stories they want to hear.

Using journalists to accomplish this goal is a new approach, largely untested by marketing and PR departments, yet I predict that the first companies to hire journalists will gain distinct advantages in their niches.

YOUR CHALLENGE: A journalist can be hired at the cost of a typical big-budget marketing campaign, which usually falls flat anyway. So take a gamble on this one—you could win big in the marketplace of ideas.

WHEN THE WORLD COMES TO YOU

As you've been reading the inspiring stories in this book, I hope you've noticed the consistent pattern. I first saw it myself as I was researching *World Wide Rave*. All the success stories we've looked at follow a similar path, a path I hope you'll soon follow: You must create some great free Web content that drives people to you. It's not about your product; it's about how you deliver great information that people pay attention to and share with their friends.

 That people come to you is the truly amazing aspect of a World Wide Rave. When the world is talking about your organization, all kinds of doors begin to open.

It doesn't matter whether you're with a big company, an entrepreneurial startup, or a nonprofit. You could be an author, a pastor, a swim coach, or a rock star. When you've got something funny, or fascinating, or amazing, or informational, the world wants to know about it—and many of the people exposed to your ideas will want to do business with you.

Lisa Genova is the author of *Still Alice*, a novel about a young woman's descent into dementia due to early-onset Alzheimer's disease. After she wrote the book and was ready to get it into the market, Genova spent a year trying to get literary agents and editors at publishing houses to speak with her. The editors all treated her as yet another aspiring writer not worth their time, and the few literary agents she managed to reach thought her novel wouldn't sell.

But Genova—who graduated as valedictorian from Bates College with a degree in bio-psychology and holds a Ph.D. in neuroscience from Harvard—knew in her gut that her story of Alice, a 50-year-old psychology professor whose initial moments of forgetfulness and confusion gradually worsen and steal pieces of her identity and self-image, would resonate with a large number of readers. "Five million people have Alzheimer's, and each has family and friends who know them and care about them," Genova says. "So I thought the market for the book could be big."

Genova had *Still Alice* all ready to go; all a publisher had to do was sign a deal. "The book was written and edited, and I had quotes for the back," she says. "I even had an author photo, and my husband designed the cover." Genova developed a *Still Alice* web site,[110] which is chock-full of information about her and the book. "I'll be the first to admit that I'm not very savvy about HTML, but I was able to make it work," she says.

[110] www.stillalice.com/

Drawing from her professional associations and on her accurate attention to detail, Genova felt confident that the book would be interesting to important groups like the National Alzheimer's Association. "In my conversations with physicians and scientists, having an understanding of the molecular biology of this disease certainly gave me the knowledge and the vocabulary to ask the right kinds of questions and the ability to understand the implications of their answers," she says. "It gave me access to the right people to talk to. My professional background gave people the credentials they needed to feel comfortable letting me in and revealing what they know." She worked with the Dementia Advocacy and Support Network and spoke daily with patients. "People with Alzheimer's stand on ground that is constantly shifting beneath their feet," she says. "Familiar symptoms get worse (more frequent or intensified) or new symptoms emerge, and so just when people think they've adapted to it all, made all the adjustments and accommodations needed, there's more work to do. This can be frustrating, exhausting, demoralizing. I see all that."

Genova reached out to the Alzheimer's Association because she was convinced that *Still Alice*, although fictional, was still a truthful and respectful depiction of life with the disease. "And it was unique in that it presented this depiction from the point of view of the person with Alzheimer's, rather than the caregiver," she says. "I thought the Alzheimer's Association might be interested in the book in some way, perhaps endorsing it, providing a link to it from their web site, etc." Genova contacted their marketing department and gave them the link to the book's web site, which was already up. They asked for a copy of the manuscript. "Soon after that, their marketing rep contacted me saying they loved the manuscript," she says. "They wanted to give it their stamp of approval and asked if I would write a blog for the nationwide Voice Open Move campaign they were launching [at the] end of that month."

The interest from the Alzheimer's Association forced Genova to make important decisions about the book, because *Still Alice* still wasn't published. "It could take years for it to find a publishing house and become available to readers," she says. "Realizing that I'd created something that the Alzheimer's Association thought was valuable—that could help educate and reassure the thousands of people trying to navigate a world with Alzheimer's—I felt an urgent responsibility to get the book out."

Genova chose to self-publish *Still Alice* with iUniverse, a print-on-demand publisher with partnerships at online retailers to sell their books. At the same time, she agreed to write the blog proposed by the Alzheimer's Association,[III] formally affiliating with the group and personally committing to donate $1 per book to Alzheimer's care and research through the association. However, her work had just begun, because once *Still Alice* was published on July 13, 2007, Genova set out to create a World Wide Rave. Her starting point was the National Alzheimer's Association endorsement. "Of all the books out there on the topic of Alzheimer's, to my knowledge, mine is the only one to have this stamp from them," she says. Her first blog post for the organization was titled "How Did I Get Here?" It describes her background as a neuroscientist and her experience with her grandmother who had Alzheimer's disease.

The natural partnership gave Genova a huge platform. "I received lots of email from people who thanked me for writing the book," she says. "For someone with Alzheimer's or a caregiver of a loved one with this, to tell me that I got it right, that it's uncanny how true it all was, that they saw themselves all over the book, well that's the highest compliment I can get."

[III] http://actionalz.org/blog

Genova became a World-Wide-Rave-generating machine. Pointing to the great information on her web site, she gained the interest of mainstream media and did countless interviews. A great book review appeared in *The Boston Globe*. She was on Fox News and National Public Radio.[112] And she participated on numerous podcasts. "I got very good at talking about my book," she says. "I could speak with confidence and efficiency, and it was generating book sales that I could measure, such as the Amazon sales results and the overwhelmingly positive reader reviews."

The idea for Genova and *Still Alice* is that a World Wide Rave plus the measurable sales success on Amazon and other online booksellers would generate buzz in the book world. "An agent contacted me and, because of my experience doing interviews, I was prepared to talk about the book," she says. "I signed with her, and *Still Alice* sold at auction in June 2008 for just over half a million dollars to Simon & Schuster." The first print run of the new edition of the book was 250,000 copies and translation rights have sold to ten foreign countries so far, with more in the works. In addition, *Still Alice* won the 2008 Bronte Prize.[113]

Yes, it was a lot of work. But what an amazing success story! One person with a self-published book who had been ignored by the entire book trade shared her enthusiasm, generating a World Wide Rave within a specific group (people who care about Alzheimer's), and the result is the fulfill-ment of a dream—the chance to share her passion for the subject with people who care—not to mention a huge book deal from a major pub-lisher. "Do I think that my web site, reviews at Amazon, my blog, inter-views on podcasts, profiles at MySpace [and sites for book lovers], and reviews of *Still Alice* at other blogs, links at my web site to traditional press on the book, all contributed to the bidding publishing houses' ability to see the market potential for *Still Alice*?" Genova asks. "I absolutely do!"

---

[112] Genova worked with Kelley and Hall Book Publicity, www.kelleyandhall.com/
[113] www.bronteprize.org/

Advice for generating a World Wide Rave

from Lisa Genova, author of *Still Alice*

"It feels like I've been trying to storm the castle of traditional publishing for more than two years. I'm bloody and sweaty. But they finally let me in, and now they are welcoming me. I know so many aspiring writers who are sitting in a holding pattern, with a work completed, waiting to find a literary agent. They're stuck, unable to give themselves permission to write the next book because they're waiting to find out if their work is 'good enough'—waiting to find out if they're a 'real writer.' This state of waiting, of not writing and self-doubt, is the worst state any writer can be in. My advice is this: If you don't find a literary agent falling into your lap quickly enough, if you feel like your work is done and is ready to be shared with the world, self-publish. Give your work to the world. Let it go.

"You absolutely have to have a web site. Get a profile up on Facebook and MySpace right away. When you get press, people will immediately want to go to your site. And link to the amazing reviews and news that comes out. Your site is your business card; it is how you show the world what you're doing. A site facilitates everything you're trying to do, and you don't need to spend thousands of dollars. You can do it yourself."

• •

STOP MAKING EXCUSES

Excuses.

I constantly hear excuses.

Marketing people have excuses for why they can't create a World Wide Rave. CEOs, company presidents, and other executives have excuses for why their particular product, service, or organization doesn't have potential to spread online. Authors and musicians offer excuses for why their books or music aren't selling. Often, the excuse comes to me like this: "But David, we're a _____. We can't do that." You can fill in the blank with your organization's excuse. I've already heard most of them: big company, small company, public company, venture-funded company, nonprofit, church, accountant, blood donation center, indie rock band, famous university, blah, blah, blah. Sorry, but they're all just excuses.

Another excuse I hear a lot these days comes from people pointing to polls and research reports that ask questions such as "Do you read blogs?" or "Do you use social media?" or "Do you go to video-sharing sites?" Often the data show rather small use compared to those who, say, use search engines or email.

This sort of data is misleading and dangerous to an organization's overall marketing and PR efforts. Why? Because it's used by resistant executives to justify sticking exclusively to the methods that worked decades ago, like image advertising, direct mail, and the Yellow Pages. I frequently hear CEOs, CFOs, and VPs of marketing say things like; "See, social media, blogs, and YouTube are not important, so we won't do them here. They're a waste of time." Other people say: "I don't read blogs, so how important are they?"

These excuses miss two tremendously important points: First, practically everyone uses Google and other search engines regularly, and the searches frequently return blog posts, YouTube videos, or other social media content high in the results. So even though people may report "no" when asked whether they use social media like blogs and video-sharing sites, nearly everyone has found this content via search.

Second, when people who are not regular users of social media ask their (non-social-media) networks for advice, they often do it via email. Frequently the answers that come back include URLs to company and product pages. And those links from friends, colleagues, or family members often include blog posts and other social media content. A mother may ask her friends a question like "What's the best baby stroller to buy?" The answer may include a link to a blog post or a site with an embedded video. Again, the person asking for advice probably didn't even know she'd been sent to a blog or video-sharing site.

 Many people who reach content via search don't know what sort of media they're enjoying! Don't let your bosses diminish the hidden value of social media as search engine fodder and as valuable sources of information that people share with their networks.

But you can produce this content only if you stop making excuses and go out and create something.

YOUR CHALLENGE: When will you stop making excuses? (Or when will you stop allowing your bosses to make excuses for you?)

WHERE THE HELL IS MATT?

Matt Harding generated one of the coolest World Wide Raves I have ever seen. You've probably seen it, too. Harding describes himself as "a 31-year-old deadbeat from Connecticut who used to think that all he ever wanted to do in life was make and play videogames." On a trip wandering around Asia several years ago, Harding was in Hanoi when a friend suggested that he film a particular silly dance that he occasionally does when the moment is right. Some time later, a friend posted the video of Matt on his blog, and people passed around a link, one to another, until a lot of people had seen it.

Fast forward to 2006. Marketing people at Stride gum[114] had seen Harding's video and contacted him, saying, "We like what you're doing. We want to help you." They agreed to sponsor a six-month trip through 39 countries and all seven continents. "In that time, I danced a great deal," Harding writes. The resulting video, which Matt posted onto YouTube himself, is called *Where the Hell is Matt?* and has been seen more than 11 million times. "I didn't do anything to promote the video myself," he says. "It was a featured video on the YouTube site, and that was the kick start. But if people don't pass it around, a video won't get a lot of views. It has to be real for people to be interested."

Harding says the key to his World Wide Rave is that it's such a simple thing that he's doing. "It makes people feel good and feel happy," he says. "The world is overwhelming and it is comforting to have something that encompasses that scope but is still really simple. It's nice to know that there is something that can link people all over the world. People want to feel good about humanity, and this helps."

[114] www.stridegum.com/

After that first trip, things settled down for a while, and then in 2007 Matt went back to Stride with another idea. "With the release of the 2006 video we created an email list on my site and invited people to sign up," Harding says. "Many people danced with me, and we showed some of that in an outtake video. I showed [the people from Stride] my inbox, which was overflowing with emails from all over the planet. I told them I wanted to travel around the world one more time and invite the people who'd written me to come out and dance, too." Stride agreed and again sponsored his journey.

"For the 2008 video, when we went to a city I used the email list and invited thousands of people to dance with me," Harding says. The resulting video, *Where the Hell is Matt? (2008)*,[115] is remarkable both for Harding and for Stride. I particularly like that the sponsor of the trip only gets a two-second "thank you" from Harding at the very end. Stride's logo did not appear throughout the video (which is what most companies would have insisted on), and he didn't do anything overt to promote the sponsor, like hold Stride gum in his hand while he danced. The product never appears, and yet the video is so powerful that you're almost compelled to watch till the end and see the credits, where Stride is finally mentioned.

The video was 14 months in the making, and it features a cast of thousands. This time, Harding visited 42 countries from Bhutan to Zanzibar and danced in all of them with enthusiastic locals. The first clip was shot in San Francisco on a cross-country road trip, and then he set out abroad. The round-the-world trip took six months and 76 airplane flights. The last clip was shot in Seattle a few days after his final landing.

[115] www.youtube.com/watch?v=zlfKdbWwruY

"When the 2008 video was released, the 10,000 people on my invite list all got a link to the video, helping to generate a lot of early views," Harding says. "There has been a lot media coverage. *The New York Times* did a story on the front page of the Arts & Leisure section, and six stills of the video were shown as photos. It was a really generous piece. That fed more media because so many members of the media read the *Times*. Lots of other stories came out and many new people went to the video."

Not only is *Where the Hell is Matt?* (2008) a smash-hit World Wide Rave (more than ten million people have seen it on YouTube and on his site),[116] it is also a worldwide production featuring a global cast. Today, Harding is planning new international travel (perhaps including some new videos), and he's working on a book based on his *Where the Hell is Matt?* adventure.

Advice for generating a World Wide Rave

from Matt Harding, star of *Where the Hell is Matt?*

"Mysteries are great. So I like to keep a sense of mystery. I leave a question in viewers' minds and don't answer the question for them in the video. Many people wonder if my video was faked [it was not]. The Stride sponsorship was also a little of a mystery, which I think is more potent than if Stride had made it more obvious that they were involved.

From my experience, sincerity is something that is impossible to fake and hard to come by but something that people respond to. Sincerity levels the playing field for independent video creators compared to large organizations. The person making something in a bedroom has more of a chance to be sincere than someone working in a big company. I can't do computer graphic effects or extravagant stuff in my videos, but I can be sincere."

....

WHAT DO YOU HAVE TO LOSE?

You don't have to be a dancing machine to have nothing to lose. Yes, it's inspiring that the Lisa Genovas and Matt Hardings of the world can reach millions and transform their lives and businesses through the power of the World Wide Rave. But even the biggest, most conservative multinational corporations will find appropriate ways to capture the power of word-of-mouse to spread their ideas in new ways and generate buzz that leads to increased sales. Hell, they might even have some fun and reconnect with their customers along the way, like IBM did.

QUIT YOUR JOB

Sometimes people tell me: "David, I've tried everything. I've explained why I want to create online content to spread my company's ideas. I've asked my bosses to read your books. I'm pointing out that we all make decisions every day based on what we find on the Web. But they still won't let me do what I know is right by working on the sort of marketing you talk about."

If you face a challenge like this, don't fret. If your company wants to hold you back from implementing the ideas in this book—after you've explained what you want to do and why—maybe you need to find a new company that will appreciate your talents. If your business life is measured exclusively in terms of ROI, then maybe the best *personal* investment you can make is in a job search. Thousands of organizations would benefit from your enthusiasm. Many company executives lament the fact that they cannot find good people to implement online marketing strategies at their companies. Your skills are in high demand. Quit your job and find a company that values them!

Many people escape the corporate salary world completely to become independent contractors. Or maybe you need to strike out on your own and build a business based on your enthusiasm. Millions of people start businesses every year. That's what Jonathan Fields did. He went from a six-figure, mega-firm Manhattan attorney to become a serial lifestyle entrepreneur, building a string of health and fitness companies that have changed the lives of thousands of people.[117] "At some point, it dawns on you that the corporate ladder is really more of a treadmill," he writes. "You run faster, work harder, climb higher, sweat more blood, and push through stifling fatigue. But, in the end, all too often, you're no freer or happier than the day you began."

Jonathan Fields wasn't satisfied with his career and he quit his job to pursue what was in his gut and in his heart. Just one of his businesses, Sonic Yoga,[118] is the top-rated yoga center in New York City.

I wasn't satisfied with my corporate career, either. I had been vice president of marketing for several publicly traded technology companies in

[117] www.careerrenegade.com/main.html
[118] www.sonicyoga.com/

the late 1990s, and even though I was making good money and was well respected by my peers, the companies I worked for didn't want to implement my pioneering ideas to reach people online with great Web content. The companies I worked with were conservative and preferred to advertise in trade magazines and invest in expensive direct-mail campaigns. So I escaped the corporate world in 2002. Today, I sit on a few company boards, write books and magazine articles, blog, speak, and run seminars on the new rules of marketing and PR. Was it scary? Sure. But I'm having a blast. And I built a successful business and sold tons of books simply by implementing the ideas that you've learned here.

I am absolutely blown away by how well the World Wide Rave works, and I feel compelled to share a few comments about how it's helped me:

- If you had Googled my full name, David Meerman Scott, around the time I started my business, you would have gotten zero hits. Now there are nearly 200,000 references, all talking about me and my ideas—and all the result of people sharing my ideas online.

- My first e-book, *The New Rules of PR: How to create a press release strategy for reaching buyers directly*,[119] has been downloaded more than 250,000 times since it was released in early 2006, and it has led directly to hundreds of thousands of dollars in speaking engagements in the past couple of years.

- I spent almost no money promoting my previous book published by John Wiley & Sons, *The New Rules of Marketing & PR*, when it came out in hardcover in 2007. Because of a World Wide Rave from more than 500 bloggers all over the planet who wrote about the book on their blogs, it became one of the most popular PR and marketing books in the world. As of this writing, the book is being translated into 20 languages.

---

[119] www.davidmeermanscott.com/documents/New_Rules_of_PR.pdf

- The power of a World Wide Rave—people sharing my ideas—led directly to members of the mainstream media finding me without me pitching them. I've had a front-page quote in the small business section of the *Wall Street Journal* and appeared on MSNBC and Fox News. I've had my ideas written about in magazines such as *BusinessWeek*, *Entrepreneur*, and *Publishers Weekly* and many newspapers such as *The Washington Post* and *The Boston Globe*, and I've been interviewed and talked about on radio shows, podcasts, and webinars. And the reporters and editors all found me—not the other way around!

Imagine how much I would have had to pay to get an equivalent number of people to pay attention via advertising, media relations, and other old-rules approaches! Millions of dollars, perhaps. Guess how much I paid: zero dollars.

You may have noticed that I started some my stories by asking what you'd do in a given situation. I followed up these hypotheticals with something along the lines of "If you're a typical X, you'd probably Y," before going on to tell you about how someone I'd interviewed had done something totally different. As you can see, the same has been true of my career. I could have stayed in the corporate world, but I didn't. When I started out on my own, I could have spent a bunch of money advertising my services and cold-calling prospects. But, as you've learned, I didn't do anything like that. Instead, I started a blog and wrote some e-books that have been shared by more than a thousand bloggers and eagerly read by hundreds of thousands of people. Isn't it wonderful that some of those people who are exposed to my ideas then *choose* to do business with me? They seek me out every day.

You can achieve these results, too, by following the ideas in this book and generating a World Wide Rave of your own.

Large or small, big corporation or entrepreneur, you and your business need to get out there and make it happen! Let's review, one more time, the Rules of the Rave:

Rules of the Rave

- **Nobody cares about your products** (except you).
- **No coercion required.**
- **Lose control.**
- **Put down roots.**
- **Create triggers that encourage people to share.**
- **Point the world to your** (virtual) **doorstep.**

I wouldn't have said it so many times if it weren't true. A World Wide Rave—having others tell and spread your story for you—is one of the most exciting and powerful ways to reach your audiences. It's not easy to harness the power, but any company with thoughtful ideas to share—and clever ways to create interest in them—can, after some careful preparation, become famous and find success on the Web.

YOUR CHALLENGE:

(This is the big one.)

HOW WILL YOU CREATE A WORLD WIDE RAVE?

YOUR CHALLENGE:

YOUR CHALLENGES (A REVIEW)

I've written this book to drive you to action. As you read it and learn from dozens of people who have achieved amazing success, your challenge is to ignore the advice of your agencies and instead think about what you can do to trigger a World Wide Rave of your own.

Consider what's interesting about you and your organization. Why do people like to do business with you? How are you unique? Those are the things that you'll leverage to tell your story directly online and trigger a World Wide Rave.

What slightly subversive (but not illegal or unethical) strategies, like encouraging people to use their mobile phones in a place where it is not normally allowed, can you use to trigger a World Wide Rave?

Get out of your nice, comfortable office and speak with members of your buyer personas. Meet them on their own turf—their home, office, or where they go for fun—and listen to their problems. Then create something interesting and valuable especially for them, and offer it for free on the Web.

Never talk about your products and services again. Instead, focus on your buyer personas and how you can solve problems for them.

E-books are a great way to dip your toes into the ocean of the World Wide Rave. If you're a thought leader—a person recognized as having innovative and important ideas—go ahead and write an e-book. I dare you. (And if you do, please send me the link!)

How can you push the envelope of what's tried and true in your market? The sex angle certainly isn't for everyone, but are there other subjects you could incorporate in your efforts that others are too scared to talk about?

You've got to think in terms of spreading ideas, not generating leads. A World Wide Rave gets the word out to thousands or even millions of potential customers. But only if you make your content easy to find and consume.

Think about how your information spreads online. If you are clamping down and exerting control, then your ideas aren't spreading as they could be. Consider what valuable content you can offer totally free.

Use Web analytics software to measure how many people are accessing the information on your site and decide whether you're satisfied with the number. If not, how can you publish something that people will want to link to? Finding the answer could dramatically increase the number of people who visit your site, thrilling your bosses in the process.

Every company has something fascinating or unique or funny that can be turned into a video that people will want to share. You do, too. What's that one thing that everyone who knows you comments about? Build your video efforts around that.

You can't generate a World Wide Rave if your employees are forbidden from accessing the sites to trigger one. If you trust your employees, they might surprise you with the ways they promote your business on social media sites. But if you don't trust them, you end up with only the corporate dregs—workers who don't mind submitting to an organization that won't let them communicate the way people do today.

Get a group together and draft a set of social media guidelines for your company. Get them approved by the legal and communications departments, and then let all employees know about the guidelines to encourage social media participation.

Think about what your organization can do to work with bloggers (as well as podcasters and video bloggers). Be the first organization in your industry to embrace them by including them in your press conferences, scheduling interviews for them with your executives, or even making them part of your product tests.

Facebook applications are all about providing an interesting way for friends to connect and share valuable information. Your business probably lends itself to an entertaining or useful application, too.

If you aren't on Facebook and Twitter already, create profiles for yourself. Do it today—it takes less than an hour to get going. Then interview your buyer personas to learn what other social networking sites are popular with them and build profiles on those sites, too.

If you're not doing it already, begin monitoring blogs, chat rooms, forums, and social networking sites for discussions about your company and its products. Set up alerts in Google and other search engines so you'll be informed immediately when you are mentioned in the blogosphere. Participate in the discussions that are already ongoing about you.

An interactive tool is frequently the perfect device for generating a World Wide Rave. Consider your own business and your expertise and then devise a clever interactive tool of your own.

Create a team and a process in advance and get internal preapprovals in place so that when a new trend breaks, you can respond very quickly. If you work for a nimble organization, an instant response to something in the news, a reaction to a change in regulations, or a clever piggyback off somebody else's World Wide Rave can be both fun and rewarding.

Think about the kinds of user-generated content that would naturally tie in with your product, and devise an online contest of your own.

Entering an online contest of some kind, perhaps one involving a video, might be just the thing to motivate you to create some compelling content. Go for it—you've got nothing to lose!

Go to Google and do a search for the important phrases that your buyers are using to find organizations like yours, and look at where you fall in the search results. Consider what great content you can publish to trigger a World Wide Rave that will get people linking to your content and send your site to the top of the search results.

What proprietary data and metrics do you have that would be valuable to others? Publish them and offer them for free to generate a World Wide Rave.

If you aren't satisfied with your search engine placement, consider what great content you can create (like a blog or an e-book or some news releases) to draw links from other people and help boost your ranking.

Take a look at your site and find a link you can flip around. Measure the traffic before and after the switch and see which version works better. Perhaps your site includes a headline like this: "How to increase productivity and drive revenue." *Yawn*. How many times have we all read something like that? How about this: "How to destabilize productivity, deter customers, and diminish revenue." Now that's likely to get some attention!

A journalist can be hired at the cost of a typical big-budget marketing campaign, which usually falls flat anyway. So take a gamble on this one—you could win big in the marketplace of ideas.

When will you stop making excuses?
(Or when will you stop allowing your bosses to make excuses for you?)

(This is the big one.)
How will *you* create a World Wide Rave?

BRAND, COMPANY, AND PEOPLE INDEX

ABOUT THE AUTHOR

David Meerman Scott is a marketing strategist, a professional speaker, and seminar leader. He's the author of the bestselling book, *The New Rules of Marketing & PR*, and three other books.

For most of his career, Scott worked in the online news business. He was vice president of marketing at NewsEdge Corporation and held executive positions in an electronic information division of Knight-Ridder, at the time one of the world's largest newspaper companies. He's also held senior management positions at an e-commerce company, been a clerk on a Wall Street bond-trading desk, worked in sales at an economic consultancy, and acted in Japanese television commercials.

Today he spends his time evangelizing the new rules of marketing and PR and how ideas spread online in keynote speeches to groups all over the world and teaching full-day workshops for companies, nonprofits, and government clients.

A graduate of Kenyon College, Scott has lived in New York, Tokyo, and Hong Kong and now lives in the Boston area.

Before this became a book, the ideas appeared on Scott's blog. See what he's thinking about now at www.WebInkNow.com, or follow him on Twitter at twitter.com//dmscott.

ACKNOWLEDGMENTS

First, a disclosure: Because I am personally active in the world that I write about in my books and blog, there are inevitably conflicts in my work. I have friends in some of the companies that I discuss in this book and I have run seminars, delivered keynotes, or consulted for several of the organizations mentioned here.

Special thanks to Matt Holt at Wiley, who understood immediately what this book could be and gave me the freedom to create it.

The following people kindly read early drafts of the book and provided valuable suggestions: Kyle Matthew Oliver, Steve Johnson, Mark Levy, Phil Myers, and Graham Joyce. Also at Wiley, thanks to Shannon Vargo, Christine Moore, Kim Dayman, Jessica Campilango, Cynthia Shannon, Peter Knapp, Rose Sullivan, Deborah Schindlar, and Lori Sayde-Mehrtens for their help and support.

This book was designed by the wonderfully talented Doug Eymer.

And, as always, thank you to Yukari and Allison.

DAVID MEERMAN SCOTT,
LIVE AT **YOUR** EVENT!

David Meerman Scott is available for keynote presentations and full-day seminars. He is a frequent speaker at tradeshows, conferences, and company events around the world.

Scott knows that sitting through a boring or off-topic speech is utterly painful. So he keeps things a bit edgy (some would say confrontational) and uses stories and humor to craft presentations that are educational, motivational, and entertaining. But whenever he is front of a group, whether of six people or six hundred, he provides valuable and action-able information about the new rules of marketing and PR, online thought leadership, and reaching buyers directly with Web content.

Visit www.DavidMeermanScott.com for more information.